Naughty Nights

By: Kevin J. Amon

Other Poetry Books

By: Kevin J. Amon

Heartbreak and Pancakes: Love On An Empty Stomach

Butterscotch and Body Slams: Wrestling With The Sweet Side

Band Aids and Barbeque: Mending The Wounded Soul

Whispers From My Mind

Untangled Moments

All books are on www.Amazon.com

Facebook: Poets dream

"DIRTY THOUGHTS DON'T COME CLEAN IN THE LAUNDRY ROOM"

K.J.A

DEAR READER,

THANK YOU FOR PURCHASING "NAUGHTY NIGHTS."

MY JOURNEY AS A WRITER BEGAN IN 1995. ALONG THE WAY, I HAVE WRITTEN MANY POEMS COVERING VARIOUS TOPICS. THIS BOOK ENCOMPASSES A NEW CONCEPT FOR ME, EROTICA. AS HUMANS, WE ALL HAVE NEEDS, WANTS AND DESIRES. IN THIS BOOK, I DELVE INTO SOME OF THOSE DEEP DESIRES, FANTASIES, AND EROTIC MOMENTS. TABOO TO SOME, SUCH PASSIONS ARE HARD TO EXPRESS.

"NAUGHTY NIGHTS" HAS 100 EROTIC POEMS THAT WILL NOT ONLY OPEN YOUR MIND, BUT HELP YOU CONVEY THOSE THOUGHTS TO THAT SPECIAL SOMEONE. I HOPE YOU ENJOY THIS PASSIONATE JOURNEY. IT'S TIME TO FEED THOSE DESIRES!!!

MANY THANKS TO YOU ALL,

KEVIN J. AMON

TABLE OF CONTENTS

HER BEEF CURTAINS -81-

EDIBLE -83-

BUBBLE BATH GIGGLES -85-

SHE WAS MY POEM -88-

OH SANTA -89-

SO YOU WANT TO FLIRT -91-

YOUR HOSTAGE -93-

DRAIN -95-

HER NAKED CANVAS -96

BAY WINDOW -97-

TAKE ME TO YOUR BED -99-

AT THE FRONT DOOR -101-

LADDER TO MY WINDOW -105-

GYM FLIRT -107-

SHE GAVE ME THAT GRIN -109-

I WANT TO BITE YOU -110-

The Other Day

It was the other day; I was vacuuming my
bedroom floor,
Within a few minutes, I noticed the opening of
my bedroom door.
My girlfriend walked in with her lusty raven
filled hair,
All she did was look at me like a vulture and
stared.
She came towards me and pulled off her top,
Her sexy tits came out and went plop.
She took the vacuum from me and threw it in
the corner,
It made me hornier!!
With the vacuum still screaming,
I thought I was dreaming.
With no words, she grabbed my cock,
Instantly it turned solid as a rock.
She dropped to her knees and my pants went
zip,
Slowly they came off my hips.
My dick was now exposed within her painted
fingernails,
My mind was rocking and drifting like sails.
She shoved my dick into her soft wet mouth,
Caressing my balls with her other hand down
south.

I FELT LIKE MY COCK WAS TOUCHING THE BACK OF
HER THROAT,
SHE MADE SEXY AND SEDUCTIVE NOISES SOUNDING LIKE
A BILLY GOAT.
SHE TRIED SPEAKING SOME ITALIAN,
THEN I GRABBED HER FACE AND FUCKED HER MOUTH
LIKE A STALLION.
SHE KNEW MY DICK WASN'T A SURPRISE,
HER MASCARA RAN BLACK DOWN FROM HER EYES.
I'M HER PREY AND IT WASN'T TRAGIC,
WATCHING MY COCK DISAPPEAR, NOTHING BUT MAGIC.
I WAS AT THE HEIGHT OF MY AROUSAL AND I
COULDN'T HOLD BACK,
SHE WANTED MY SWEET COME FROM THIS MIDDAY
SNACK.
I TOLD HER I WAS CLOSE AND SHE SUCKED SOME
MORE,
DOWN HER THROAT MY SAUCE WENT TO HER CORE.
SHE TOLD ME, "THAT WAS SO YUMMY,"
STANDING OVER ME JUST RUBBING HER TUMMY!!!

Join Me

Join me!
Don't be afraid
Leave all your worries behind
I will be waiting for you
Come alone
Your fantasies will belong to me
Enter slowly
Enjoy the candle glare
I will be seated above
Be careful
Watch out for my teeth
My hunger is dripping down my chin
Leave your clothes at the bottom of the stairs
Walk to me
Let your eyes join mine in this mental dance
Focus on this sacred cave
Worry no more
Grab my hand
Please sit
Tell me your name?
Why are you here?
Your body looks starved for love
Do you need love to rejuvenate your soul?
Here is a pen and paper
Glide your fantasies down here with this ink
Don't be nervous
Let your oceans of desires flow into your mind
I will penetrate your thoughts with my lust

SPEAK NOW OR LEAVE UNLOVED
MY FANGS ARE EMERGING
I'M READY TO TASTE YOUR SOUL

CHOCOLATE BEAUTY

I ENJOY HAVING MY EYES IN YOUR DIRECTION,
DAY DREAMING ABOUT GIVING YOU ALL MY AFFECTION.
LINGERING DIRTY THOUGHTS JUST MOUND,
WISHING YOUR CHOCOLATE WRISTS WERE BOUND.
I WISH I CAN TAKE YOU INTO MY FANTASY,
FULFILLING MY DESIRES INTO ECSTASY.
JUST TASTING YOUR JUICY RED LIPS,
MAKING PASSIONATE LOVE SWAYING AT OUR HIPS.
YOU ALWAYS KEEP ME IN A TRANCE,
EVEN THOUGH, I WILL NEVER HAVE A CHANCE.
BUT YOU INTRIGUE MY MIND,
GETTING ALL MY NAUGHTY THOUGHTS IN A BIND.
PLEASE STOP SMILING AT ME!
MY INNER BEAST WANTS TO BREAK FREE.
I'LL JUST KEEP YOU AS MY EYE CANDY,
EVERY TIME WE PASS, I GET TO SEE.
NOTHING COULD EVER BE,
BUT YOUR SENSUAL CHOCOLATE SKIN MAKES MY MIND
FLEE.
INTO A FANTASY LAND,
YOU'RE JUST PUTTY IN MY HANDS.
YOU ALWAYS REALLY MAKE MY DAY,
GIVING ME MANY WORDS FOR THIS PAPER TO PLAY.
YOU'RE ADMIRED LET'S SAY THE LEAST,
YOU LOOK SO DELICIOUS, A BEAUTIFUL CHOCOLATE
FEAST.

WHISPERS

Drain your mind into my ears
Tell me all your thoughts
I won't bite
This is our secret
Don't be afraid
Make your words a reality
Show me what you mean
Join me in my candle lit bedroom
Remove your thoughts and display them on my body
Use your mind as your weapon
Let's make magic tonight
Tell me those whispers again
Show me exactly what you said
Word for word
Slow and steady
Let's make these whispers come to life

BITE MY LIPS

COME TO ME BABY AND BITE MY LIPS,
WATCH MY DESIRE GROW WITH MY PERKY NIPS.
TASTE MY LIPS SOAKED IN THIS SWEET WINE,
CLIMB ON ME AND LET'S TWIRL AROUND LIKE VINES.
CONNECT WITH ME TO SEE WHERE THINGS MAY GO,
WHAT DO YOU WANT ME TO SHOW?
DO YOU LIKE THIS CANDLE GLOW?
I SEE YOUR TOWER STARTING TO GROW,
BUSTING THROUGH YOUR PANTS, WHERE DO YOU WANT
IT TO GO?
I SEE YOUR EYES CANVASSING MY LAND,
FIDGETING AROUND NERVOUSLY WITH YOUR HANDS.
TOUCH ME BABY, DON'T BE SHY,
WHEN I'M DONE WITH YOU, YOU WILL BE HIGH.
HIGH OFF MY SEDUCTIVE LOOK,
JUST FOR YOU TO WRITE A POEM ABOUT ME IN YOUR
BOOK.
WHY ARE YOU SHAKING FROM YOUR CORE?
HERE, I WILL START THINGS OFF WITH MY CLOTHES ON
THE FLOOR.
I KNOW YOUR TOWER WANTS TO PLAY,
NO SECRETS ARE LEFT, JUST COME MY WAY.
DO YOU LIKE THE WAY I'M DISPLAYED?
PLEASE DON'T BE AFRAID.
I'M READY SO BRING OVER YOUR COCK,
LET'S HAVE SOME FUN AND LET THIS BOAT ROCK!

Chocolate Fix

Come here baby and get your chocolate fix,
Look into my eyes and watch my lips.
Don't I look splendid in this chocolate batter?
Oh baby! What's the matter?
Don't you just want to lick my skin?
Where do you want to begin?
Please let's share this chocolate,
You will savor this night if you just taste a
bit!
Creamy, smooth, and oh so yum,
Watch slowly as I liccccck my thumb.
Mmmm.
Is this your fantasy?
Is your brain turning to ecstasy?
Do you just want to continue to stare?
Chocolate is on me everywhere!
Come to me and do as you please,
Next I will serve your banana split down on my
knees.
Please help me clean up this mess,
Doesn't your tongue want to taste this?
I'm dripping all over this floor,
I'm the reward, from this delicious chore.
My finger is motioning you here baby,
Lick me all night and taste my chocolate gravy!

Candle Lit Bath

Steam rose from the open faucet
Bubbles gathered together
Heat filled the air
Her body slipped inside the tub
Her skin was surrounded by relaxation
I sat on the edge
Watching the candles glow in her midnight eyes
My hands opened the kinks in her neck
Moans of satisfaction stirred
Her eyes closed into bliss
Nothing but happiness she felt
The chilled wine stares at us
Two glasses are poured
Enjoying a glass together
Laughing and giggling
She watched me give her a bath
Sipping at her wine making the demands
Enjoying her pretty painted toes peeking from
the water
The bath continues
Her mind drifts away.......

DOORWAY

I WOKE UP TO HER STANDING IN THE DOORWAY
I THOUGHT I WAS IN A DREAM
HER DESIRE ESCORTED HER EYES TO MY BODY
LIKE A VULTURE
MY SKIN TINGLED
MY BODY AWAKENED
SHE WALKED SLOWLY TOWARDS ME
MY BLANKETS WRINKLED IN ANTICIPATION
SHE STRADDLED MY BODY
MY ERECTION GREETED HER THIGHS
HER BRA CAME UNDONE
HER BREASTS GREETED MY EYES
SOFT AND VOLUPTUOUS
MY HANDS ROAMED TO TOUCH HER
BREATHES WERE GETTING DEEPER
I BIT HER NECK TO CLAIM HER
I FELL INSIDE HER
RUMBLING THE WATER BED
THRASHING LIKE ALLIGATORS
HEARTS BEATING ON OVERLOAD
THE ROOM GETS DIZZY
SPINNING ON THIS OCEAN LOVE
EXPIRED BODIES WITH NO REGRETS

Satin Sheets

Warmth filtered the room
Candles were dancing along the walls
She was naked in the satin sheets
A vision of colorful beauty
My eyes danced all over her body
I started writing poetry on her skin
My tongue was the feathered pen
Spilling my words on her delicious canvas
My saliva stained ink marks penetrated her
flesh
She moaned at each stroke of my words
Delivering pleasant feelings through her brain
She squirmed like a spring time worm
Her movements were like an ocean
I finished writing my poem completing my
thoughts
She laid there in the soft sheets motionless
I said my words and she felt each one

Sweet Nectar

Her sweet nectar trickled down her inner
thighs,
Watching her body move like an ocean and rise.
Sweat beaded on her tight tummy,
Sipping on her sweet sauce, savory and yummy.
She moaned softly and pulled at my hair,
Licking her smooth lips, so pretty and bare.
Her stomach rose and sank,
Her emotional sighs were the sounds of thanks.
Several kisses and licks pounded her legs,
Moaning for more she begs.
She wanted me inside her slow and deep,
To hit an emotional high with benefits to reap.
My aching tower wiggled around her soft folds,
Biting her lips saying "you're so bold."
I entered her and she let out a huge sigh,
Reaching over her head trying to touch the sky.
Slow and steady, it was a precious dream,
Mixing emotion and love with passionate cream.
Sweat beading and glistening around,
Deep breathes of love making sounds.
The desire was tipping at its final peak,
Hands groping everything we seek.
Explosions erupted from a high to a low,
Paralyzed in passion and nowhere to go.
Connected together from this passionate dance,
Grinning together at a foggy glance.

PLEASE LEAVE A MESSAGE

PLEASE LEAVE A MESSAGE AFTER THE TONE,
"HI BABY, IT'S ME, I'M SO ALONE.
PLEASE COME OVER AND UNLEASH YOUR BEAST,
I'M NAKED IN MY BED AND I WANT TO FEAST.
I WISH YOU WOULD ANSWER THIS DAMN PHONE,
MY MOUTH IS OPEN, READY FOR YOUR BONE.
I'M JUST HERE TOUCHING MYSELF,
THERE IS A BOTTLE OF WINE JUST SITTING ON THE
SHELF.
I HAVE CANDLES DANCING AND THE MUSIC IS SET,
IT'S RAINING OUTSIDE AND I'M SO WET.
OH BABY! I HAVE HAND CUFFS WITH KEYS,
JUST KNOCK ON MY DOOR AND I WILL BE ON MY
KNEES.
PLEASE!
I HOPE YOU GET YOU THIS MESSAGE SOON,
MY FINGERS ARE SWIPING MY CLIT LIKE A BRISTLE
BROOM.
IT FEELS OH SO GOOD!
I NEED YOUR STIFF WOOD.
I BET IT TASTES SO GOOD,
I WOULD LOVE TO CRAWL THOUGH THIS PHONE IF I
COULD.
I'M NOT SURE HOW MUCH MORE I CAN WAIT,
PLEASE DON'T BE LATE.
ARE YOU COMING?
MY BODY IS NUMBING!
I WISH YOU WERE HERE TO TASTE MY SWEET SAUCE,

SO I COULD CALL YOU THE BOSS.
TO GIVE MY ASS A GOOD TOSS,
SO WE CAN EXPLODE TOGETHER
AT OUR LUSTFUL COST."

BLIND FOLDED

SHE TOOK MY HAND AND WALKED ME UPSTAIRS,
INTO THE BEDROOM SAT A SINGLE CHAIR.
CANDLES DANCED AROUND,
THE SMELL OF ROSE PETALS CANVASSED THE GROUND.
SOFT MUSIC WAS ON DISPLAY,
I'M ABOUT TO BE THE PREY.
I'M FORCED TO SIT IN THE CHAIR,
FINGERS RAKED THROUGH MY HAIR.
DARKNESS COVERED MY EYES,
NOW I'M IN DISGUISE.
HER HEELS WALKED AWAY,
I HAD NOTHING TO SAY.
MOMENTS LATER MY HANDS GET TIED TO THE CHAIR,
MY HEART WAS RACING, AND HER PERFUME KISSED
THE AIR.
I SAT THERE AND WAITED,
I WAS ELATED.
I WAS SITTING ALONE,
I HEARD NO TONE.
BUT A GRACIOUS SIGH AND MOAN.
HEELS CAME TOWARDS ME,
I WANTED TO SEE!
MY BLIND FOLD FINALLY WAS REMOVED,
STUNNED, SHOCKED AND I APPROVED.
SHE STRADDLED MY SPACE,
HER BEAUTIFUL BREASTS WERE IN MY FACE.
SHE GRINDED ON MY SOFT SLACKS,
MY UNDERWEAR CAME UNDER ATTACK.

WE KISSED IN THE HEAT OF PASSION,
IN SUCH A BEAUTIFUL FASHION.
SHE SMELLED LIKE GOLD,
I JUST WANTED TO HOLD.
BUT I WAS STILL TIED,
TO BREAK FREE, I TRIED!
HER BUTT WAS LIKE A PEACH,
MY EYES STARTED TO PREACH.
IT WAS BEYOND MY REACH,
ALL I COULD DO WAS SCREECH!
I TRIED!
I INTERNALLY CRIED,
MY BRAIN WAS FRIED.
HER MOVES GOT ME STIFF AND WET,
BUT WITHOUT REGRET!
HER TITS AND MY LIPS GRACIOUSLY MET,
I WAS THE ONE TIED UP, AS A RESULT OF A LOST BET!

Office Eyes

I can always smell her coming down the halls,
My secretary who takes all my calls.
She is so sexy; it drives me up the wall,
I can never focus because her body is what I
want to maul!!
She makes me hot in her short skirts,
At the coffee maker with the way she flirts.
I wish I could roll around with her in the dirt,
And tie her up with my shirt!
Her breasts always pop out of her top,
My brain tells me to stop!
Looking!
Because my thoughts are cooking.
I want to be intertwined like vines,
Kissing and kneading her sexy behind.
It's impossible since we are both married,
But our flirtatious minds already carried.
I can't help these wandering eyes,
I want to give her my surprise.
She makes me so weak!
My underwear always leaks.

Doorstep Kiss

It was a few nights ago at my doorstep,
After our kiss, I sat there and wept.
Knowing his lips will be the last time I touch,
How I'm in love with him so much.
A relationship I could never see,
For him to be with me.
Betrayed every time,
Only wishing he could just be mine.
We spent the last year in bliss,
From now on, I will have loneliness.
I knew exactly what the relationship was,
But I needed his desire just because.
I was new in town, I knew him only,
I didn't want to be lonely.
Now the fantasy is over and he's gone,
Mascara tears roll on the ground and into the
lawn.
It's time for bed,
This headache is twisting my head.
Tomorrow I will dread,
Knowing that this relationship is over and he's
not in my bed.
Next week he's moving away with his wife,
Keeping me on the side was just his double life!

Aquamarine

Join me in this water of aquamarine,
A serene place that has to be seen.
In this earth's nature scene,
Between these mountains of green.
"Come on babe what are you waiting for?
I'm naked to; throw your clothes on the sandy
floor.
You can see everything in this beautiful water,
Smooth and silky like butter.
Thanks for joining me with for this skinny dip,
Wrap your arms around me and kiss my lips.
Let's dance in this mystical atmosphere,
Let your fears go and let's glide together out
here.
Feel my wet skin together with yours,
Please kiss me some more.
This romance can open up new doors,
A moment of happiness and furthermore."
We dance together in this water of blue,
The sights and sounds so beautiful too.
Birds soar and stretch their wings,
Little birds tweet and sing.
This moment is so special there was no way we
could resist,
We shared a more intimate passion of bliss.
We connected, rocked back and forth creating
more waves,
Our bodies certainly craved.

Trees on the land moved and waved,
Our hearts full of desire and brave.
Moans and sighs,
Baby blue skies.
Waves crash,
Bodies thrash.
Our eyes roll back into our head,
Our bodies fall over heavy as lead.
Panting like we had a good run,
A beautiful moment created under the sun.

FUCKED WITH HER EYES

SHE LIED ON THE BED
WATCHING ME
SLOWLY PULLING HER CLOTHES OFF
ONE BY ONE
HER EYES TASTED MY FLESH
AS HER FINGER WENT IN BETWEEN HER LEGS
SOFT MOANS ECHOED
I WALKED BACK AND FORTH
I FELT LIKE PREY
THINKING ABOUT HER NAUGHTY THOUGHTS
MY UNDERWEAR THICKENED
SMELLING HER AROUSAL
SOFT SLIPPERY NOISES CANVASSED THE ROOM
I COME CLOSE TO HER
GENTLY TOUCHING HER CHIN FOR A KISS
WE LOCK EYES
HER HANDS ROAM
ON MY TOWER
STANDING TALL
MY UNDERWEAR LOWERS
AS HER LIPS GREET MY ERECTION
HER WET LIPS AND TONGUE
SATURATED MY COCK
SALIVA SPILLS ONTO HER TITS
AS I ROCK BACK AND FORTH
TO THE BACK OF HER THROAT

I Greeted Her

I greeted her with my erection
Her lips kissed my stalk
Back and forth like a type writer
I moaned
Her cheeks were stretching
Mascara was jogging down her face
She played with her flower
Wet and juicy
Her fingers were glistening
She inserted them in my mouth
Tasting her flavors of love
She pulled her panties to the side
I sank right in
Moaning in sighs
Thunder crashed between us
Volcanic eruptions exploded
Our bodies lay motionless
Juice leaking everywhere

MY WINDOW

THROW A ROCK AT MY WINDOW,
I WILL BE IN MY ROOM, READY FOR OUR SHOW.
SMACK!!
"HEY YOU, SSSHHHHH YOU NEED TO WHISPER,
BE QUIET FOR OUR FORBIDDEN DESIRES TO BE SECURE.
GRAB THAT LADDER OVER THERE,
IF YOU WANT TO SEE MY BREASTS THAT ARE BARE.
MY PARENTS ARE HOME,
SO MAKE SURE YOU'RE QUIET AND UNKNOWN!"
STEP BY STEP HE MAKES IT TO MY WINDOW,
FROM THE LOOK ON HIS FACE, HIS CROTCH IS GROWING
BELOW.
"FINALLY YOU MADE IT,
NOW KISS ME EVERYWHERE AND LEAVE TRACES OF
YOUR SPIT.
TOUCH ME IN PLACES THAT YOU TOLD ME ABOUT,
SHHHHHH DON'T BE SO LOUD!
DAMMIT SOMEONE'S COMING,
GET IN THE CLOSET AND STOP HUMMING."
"HI MOM, I'M JUST GETTING READY FOR BED,
EVEN THOUGH I WAS THINKING ABOUT GIVING MY
BOYFRIEND HEAD.
I WILL BE UP EARLY ENOUGH,
TO DO ALL OUR PLANS AND STUFF.
GOODNIGHT MOM!"
"HEY SILLY, GET OUT OF THERE,
GRAB MY TITS, DON'T STARE.
GO SIT IN THE CHAIR AND REMOVE YOUR PANTS,

THIS IS YOUR LAST CHANCE!
I DON'T HAVE LONG,
LET ME TASTE YOUR DICK WHILE HUMMING A SONG.
WOW, HE LOOKS REALLY CHUBBY TONIGHT,
GIVE ME A SECOND AND HE WILL GO OUT OF SIGHT!
MMMMM, HOW DOES THAT FEEL?
NOW YOU'RE MINE ON MY REEL.
IN AND OUT OF MY WET MOUTH,
I LOVE GOING DOWN ON YOU, DOWN SOUTH.
OH MY GOOOOOOOOD!
GEEZ, ALREADY DONE?
WAS MY MOUTH THAT MUCH FUN?
OH HUN!
YOU COULD HAVE CREAMED MY HOT BUNS.
LITTLE EXCITED TONIGHT?
OH WELL, NEXT TIME IT WILL BE MY NIGHT!
YOU BETTER GET GOING,
I THINK IT'S STILL SNOWING.
THE STREETS ARE GLOWING.
THE COLD AIR IS SHOWING.
GET OUT I SAID,
BEFORE I'M GROUNDED OR DEAD.
MY PARENTS DON'T ALLOW BOYS IN MY ROOM,
EVEN THOUGH YOUR ENTIRE NUT WENT **BOOM!**
I WILL SEE YOU TOMORROW IN ENGLISH CLASS,
I'LL LET YOU CHEAT ON MY TEST, SO YOU CAN PASS.
GOODBYE,
DAMMIT! I THINK YOU GOT SOME IN MY EYE!"

STICKY FINGERS

HER BED WAS GETTING THAT MUCH COLDER,
SHE WAS WAITING ON HER MAN TO HOLD HER.
SHE LOOKED OUT THE WINDOW AT THE MOON,
LISTENING TO HER MESSAGE "I'LL BE HOME SOON."
HER MIND STIRRED AND THE NIGHT WAS RUNNING,
SHE WAS IN SEXY LINGERIE AND WAS STUNNING.
LACE DANCED ALL OVER HER SKIN,
ANTICIPATING A NIGHT OF LOVE TO BEGIN
MINUTES PAST THAN TURNED INTO ANOTHER HOUR,
ANOTHER PEAK OUT THE WINDOW TO SCOUR.
SHE RETURNED BACK TO THE BED,
HORNY THOUGHTS RAN THROUGH HER HEAD.
CANDLES WERE DANCING JUST WATCHING HER MOVE,
HER HANDS TICKLED HER BODY IN EVERY GROOVE.
HER SMOOTH SKIN GLOWING FROM THE CANDLES,
HER HANDS PLAYED ENOUGH TO HANDLE.
HER TOP CAME OFF AND HIT THE GROUND,
GRABBING AT HER BREASTS, HER RHYTHM WAS SOUND.
MOANS AND SIGHS,
LIVING ON AN EMOTIONAL HIGH.
THE PHONE RANG AND SHE JUMPED,
HER HEART THUMPED!
WRONG NUMBER,
SHE WONDERED.
SHE WIGGLED HER PANTIES ONTO THE FLOOR,
HER RAW EMOTIONS WERE GRABBING ON MORE.
SHE SUNK INTO HER BED AGAIN,
WONDERING IF AND WHEN?

WILL HER MAN COME HOME?
HER EYES CLOSED AND HER FINGERS MADE IT PAST
HER TUMMY,
YUMMY.
ANTICIPATING A TICKLE,
SHE GIGGLES.
HER MIND IN HER EMOTIONAL DREAM,
HER LIPS FILL TO MOIST CREAM.
SOAKING AT HER THOUGHTS,
THE RIVER BROUGHT.
A FINGER GOT LOST AND THEN TWO,
SHE COULDN'T HOLD BACK SHE WENT THROUGH.
HER FINGERS CAME OUT GLISTENING,
A DOWNSTAIRS DOOR SLAMMED NOW SHE WAS
LISTENING.
SHE SLAMMED HER KNUCKLES IN MORE,
FORGETTING THE DOOR.
SHE'S DETERMINED TO FINISH THE CHORE,
MORE, MORE, MORE.
UUUUHHHH GUSH!
SHE TURNS TO MUSH,
A RIVER RUSH,
A SOFT BED, PILLOWS OF PLUSH.
THE BEDROOM DOOR OPENS, HER MAN LINGERS,
"BABY!! YOU ARE SO LATE, WANT TO LICK MY STICKY
FINGERS"?

COME TO ME

"Good evening sweetheart, please come to me,
Looks like you made your mind up and you
wanted to break free.
Please don't worry, I promise I won't bite,
Just maybe a little nibble tonight!
Come join me in this hot tub,
I know your day was long; do you need a back
rub?
I have two glasses of wine,
Please come over here beautiful you look so
fine.
Take off your clothes and leave them on the
concrete,
I don't want you to mess them up if you start
to secrete.
Wow you look so stunning all nice and bare,
Please hop inside here and share.
I don't want to stare,
I want a close up of our bodies to compare.
Are you nervous? Please don't be,
It's just you and me.
Come closer and sit on my lap,"
Our eyes locked and became a map.
Heavy kissing roared,
Hearts floored!
Bodies adored!
"Baby please sit down on my screaming erection,"
Finally making a secure connection.

OUR BODIES CAME TOGETHER,
THRASHING MAKING THIS WHITE WATER BETTER.
THE MOON PROVIDING THIS PERFECT SPOTLIGHT,
OUR FACES TOGETHER IN PURE DELIGHT.
THRUSTING KNOCKING ALL THE WATER OUT,
SIGHS, TREMORS AND SCREAMS ABOUT.
EXPLOSIONS ERUPTING FROM OUR SOULS,
GASPING FOR AIR THIS LOVE MAKING STOLE.
DANGLED BODIES SLUMPED OVER AND AROUND,
FOG EMITS SLOWLY CREEPING ON THE GROUND.

If She Was A Drink

If she was a drink, she would be a glass of red wine,
Because she is beautiful, elegant and fine.
With a full red body,
Such a hottie.
I would savor every last drop,
And I wouldn't stop.
I would nurture her taste on my lips,
Feel her liquid dance down to my hips.
I would swirl around her beautiful mind,
Touching her soul wouldn't be hard to find.
Every sip,
Would stay on my lip.
Until it drips,
And I grip!
Her inner thighs,
By surprise.
Looking me in the eyes,
Moans she cries!
Her tasty wine flows down her leg,
I beg!
Licking up the mess I created,
The wine was beautiful and not out dated.

MY PLEASURE

SHE IS SO FINE,
LIKE A GLASS OF RED WINE.
SHE IS MINE,
HER CURVES INTERTWINE.
NAKED BEFORE ME,
MY EYES BROKE FREE.
MY MIND TURNED RATED "R"
INSIDE MY CAR.
HER PANTIES CAME DOWN,
MY FACE LOOKED LIKE A CLOWN.
IT WAS SURREAL,
HER BOTTOM LIPS I WANTED TO STEAL.
SHE STRADDLED MY FACE,
WE CONNECTED WITH MY TONGUE TO PUSSY EMBRACE.
HER FACE WENT NUMB,
SHE STARTED SUCKING HER THUMB.
HER STOMACH MOVED,
MY TONGUE PROVED!
SHE WAS MELTING DOWN MY NECK,
SLURP, SIP, NOTHING TO NEGLECT.
STREAMS OF PASSION GLISTENED,
I LISTENED.
TO HER MOANS IN DELIGHT,
HER BODY SANK ON MINE WITHOUT A FIGHT!

24 HOURS

I WISH I HAD 24 HOURS WITH YOU,
I HAVE SO MANY BOTTLED UP FEELINGS TO GET
THROUGH.
I NEED TO RELEASE MY FANTASY,
BRINGING MY MIND TO A BOILING POINT INTO ECSTASY
I WOULD ENJOY EVERY MINUTE OF OUR TIME,
WE WOULD SHINE!
GLISTENING FROM THE SWEETEST KISSING,
OUR HEARTS WOULDN'T BE MISSING.
ASK ME FOR ANYTHING AND I WILL DELIVER,
I WILL MAKE YOUR MIND AND BODY QUIVER.
IT WILL BE A JOYFUL AND LUSTFUL GAME,
A CONNECTION TOGETHER SAYING OUR NAMES.
WE WOULD MAKE A MEMORY OF BLISS,
BY ENJOYING EVERY MINUTE OF THIS.
TELL ME WHEN YOU WANT BLOOD TO PASS THROUGH
YOUR VEINS
I WILL PUNISH YOUR SORROW AWAY AND MAKE
HAPPINESS REGAIN.

Go To Your Room

Go to your room
Drop your clothes on the floor
I can't wait to see your sultry body
When I open this door
Looking at your
Goose bumps rise
Your naked skin
Just for my eyes
Lay down under the candles
Soak into my bed
I want to scan over your contours
Naughty things erupt in my head
My fangs get loose
My tongue wants to play
It's ready to dance on your skin
A physical poem I want to display
Kisses drop
Your spine starts to quiver
Moans emit pleasure
My tongue enters and delivers
Inside your flower
Jack hammering away
My hair being pulled
Fuck me are words you say
My tower grows
As you slither into the tub
Your mind devoured by my pleasure
I have a handful of beautiful breasts to rub

OH BABY! PLEASE!
I WANT YOU TO FINISH ME
MY BODY IS SHAKING
I WANT YOUR PHYSICAL POETRY
I CAN'T TAKE THIS ANY LONGER
PLEASE PUT IT IN
NOW I UNDERSTAND
WHY YOU ALWAYS GIVE ME A GRIN

Igniting My Desire

Talking to you ignites my fire,
My body is trembling on my thoughts and
desires.
Your words make me a chaotic mess,
I want to ravish your sultry body and show
you my best.
I want to taste every inch of your skin,
Tell me where to begin?
I just want to nibble,
On your bodies kibble.
I want to see your stomach ripple,
I will keep things beautiful and simple.
Just let out a sigh,
And look to the sky.
You're definitely not dry.
Can we become one element?
Dream away and become heaven sent?
I want your body to be spent,
And my image in your brain with a dent.
Let's enjoy this slow motion,
Moving like a low tide in the ocean.
It's a great notion,
Is this love potion?

CAN I SHARE YOUR BED

MAY I PLEASE SHARE YOUR BED?
JUST TO HAVE A RESTING PLACE FOR MY HEAD.
MY PILLOW IS JUST FILLED WITH TEARS,
AN UNLOVED SOUL FOR MANY YEARS.
IS YOUR LIFE DOING OK?
OR IS IT LIKE MINE WITH A RAINY DISPLAY.
I WILL STAY ON MY SIDE AND YOU STAY ON YOURS,
UNLESS YOU WANT TO OPEN A PASSIONATE DOOR.
I HOPE YOU DO SLEEP WELL,
YOU ARE TIRED AS YOU ALWAYS TELL.
I WON'T CAUSE YOU ANY PAIN,
I JUST HOPE MY EYES DURING THE NIGHT DON'T TURN
TO RAIN.
I WILL JUST LAY HERE AND WATCH THE MOON,
I WILL BE GONE TOMORROW SOMETIME BEFORE NOON.
I WON'T MAKE ANY MESS,
BUT I MIGHT CONFESS.
IF I LAY A KISS ON YOUR CHEEK,
THAT'S ALL I WILL SPEAK.
FOR NOW, I MUST TRY AND FALL ASLEEP,
SO I WON'T HERE MYSELF WEEP.
EXCUSE ME MISS?
COULD I GIVE YOU A PASSIONATE GOOD NIGHT KISS?

Bubble Bath

May I draw you up a bubble bath?
Can I sit on the tub just to talk and laugh?
I will set out some candles ablaze,
Just to relax your tiring day.
How about having a glass of wine?
Something nice to relax your mind.
Do you mind if I play with your hair?
Look into your eyes that are so pretty to
stare.
Do you need your back rubbed?
How are those bubbles in the tub?
Anything else you need?
Ask me and I'll do any deed.
Do you mind if I slip out of my jeans?
Because I need to get clean.
To clean off my dirty dream.
Ahhhh nice and warm,
You look so precious in the wet form.
Could I come closer and near?
Do you fear?
My attraction to your pretty soul,
It's your words that my mind stole.
Do you mind if I give you a kiss?
This is so romantic inside here with an
abundance of bliss.
One plus one, you do the math.
Can we create a new path?
Join me, please come close,

STOP WIGGLING YOUR NOSE.
I KNOW YOU WANT ME,
LET'S JUST BREAK FREE.
IT WILL MAKE OUR CURRENT SITUATION A LITTLE MORE
AT EASE,
WILL YOU MAKE LOVE TO ME.........PLEASE?

Italian Class

I remember well my 10th grade Italian class,
I had the sexiest teacher with a perfect little
peach ass.
She had long curly brown hair down to her
lower back,
Drool came from my mouth and my hormones
were under attack.
Her body was slim and she wore tight clothes,
Smelled so great and her essence went up my
nose.
Her name was Miss Rizutti,
She was an absolute cutie!
She always caught me in a naughty day dream,
My underwear was melting and I was making
cream.
She would call my name to answer a question,
But my hormones were raging and I had a
nervous complexion.
She always made my sit in front of the class,
Why would I pass?
A clear view of her soft chest and ass!
There were times she would sit on my table,
Thunder would rumble in my pants and I was
unstable.
She would call me by my last name, "Hey Amon,"
But I treated her in my mind like a tasty
cinnabon!
Just dreaming and staring through her clothes,

SMELLING HER BEAUTY THROUGH MY NOSE.
SHE DROVE ME INSANE,
WITH MANY UNDERWEAR STAINS.
I WAS ALWAYS IN PAIN,
FROM BONERS I GAINED.
DURING CLASS I HAD THE MOST EMBARRASSING
MOMENT EVER,
I THOUGHT I WAS A GENIUS AND VERY CLEVER.
IT WAS A DAY OUR CLASS WAS TAKING A TEST,
I MET EYES WITH A FRIEND AND PHYSICALLY GESTURED
"LOOK AT MISS RIZUTTI'S BIG CHEST."
BUT I GOT CAUGHT AND IT WAS A BIG SURPRISE,
MISS RIZUTTI WAS SHOCKED LOOKING ME IN THE
EYES.
MY FACED TURNED BRIGHT RED,
HER EYES GREW BIG AND HER HANDS COVERED HER
HEAD.
I THOUGHT I WAS DEAD,
LOOKING AT HER FACE I STARTED TO DREAD.
I STARTED SWEATING INSIDE MY CLOTHES,
TAPPING MY FEET AND TOES.
THE TEST WAS FINALLY OVER AND THE BELL RANG,
MY HEART WAS POUNDING AND IT SANG.
NERVOUS AND SHAKING MISS RIZUTTI TOOK MY TEST,
SCARED TO EVEN LOOK INTO HER EYES AT BEST.
SHE LOOKED AT ME AND GAVE ME A GRIN,
SHIVERING WITH ANXIETY, LOOKS LIKE SHE WAS
FLATTERED BY MY LITTLE SIN!!!!

TRUE STORY!!!!

Play With Me

Please stay and play,
You are my featured prey.
My delicious display,
Can I look at you naked if I may?
My thoughts of you are tired,
Lusting over you I desire.
I'm tired of just admiring,
My pistons are shaking and my gears are firing.
Let me just light this candle,
Enough for our eyes to handle.
Let's make animal shapes on the walls,
Scratching at our skin with our paws.
We have a lot of love to toss.
Teach me things, please, **BOSS!**
Enter me,
Don't make me plea.
Our minds agree,
Don't you see?
I'm soaking wet,
Just let,
Everything go,
Take it slow.
Let's make a show,
Wrap your legs around me like a bow.
How does that feeeeeel?
A wonderful wet pleasurable meal!!
My heart is yours to steal,
I can't believe my dreams became real!

TATTOO ME

TATTOO ME WITH YOUR FRAGRANT KISS,
EVERY INCH OF MY BODY, PLEASE DON'T MISS.
I NEED THIS,
ELEVATE MY MIND TO A NEW BLISS.
PLEASE LEAVE MARKS SO I CAN SEE,
EVERY BIT OF LOVE YOU TATTOOED IN ME.
DON'T BE GENTLE; I WANT YOU TO BITE,
GIVE ME EVERYTHING YOU HAVE TONIGHT.
SLAY ME LIKE A VAMPIRE,
I'M ALL YOURS TO DESIRE.
HOUR AFTER HOUR,
MY BODY WILL REMAIN SWEET AND NOT SOUR.
I WILL TRICKLE WITH FLOWING JOY,
PLAY WITH ME, I'M YOUR TOY.
BOY!
I'M FEELING YOUR FANGS,
YOU HAVE DEEP HUNGER PANGS.
I LOVE HOW I'M YOUR PREY,
DIZZY AND DRUNK, I DON'T KNOW WHAT TO SAY.
I LOVE THIS EMOTIONAL HIGH,
I'M IN THE SKY!
CONTINUE WITH THIS LOVE FELT TATTOO,
MAKE ME BEAUTIFUL COLORS, BLACK AND BLUE!

Photo

I looked into her eyes
She looked at mine
She's so beautiful
I wrapped around her like a vine
My mind moved
In all directions
Fireworks in my brain
I gave her my affection
Her sultry look
Her smooth soft skin
Took over my mind
That's where I had a mental sin
I made love to her
My eyes were full of steam
Emotions ran
But it was just a dream
She's so precious
Like a beautiful flower
Her looks are so desirable
Her delicious eyes had that power

On The Hood Of Her Car

She pushed me backwards
On the hood of her Camaro
Whispering in my ears
Sweet sounds like sparrows
She pushed herself on me
Biting my bottom lip
Told me to grab her
I grabbed her at her hips
Her hands were wandering
Slowly around my crotch
I got really nervous
I started to look at my watch
I was pushed back more
Fully lying on my back
She rips off her top
My eyes view her beautiful tender snacks
Like a bully
She pins me down
Kisses flying on my neck
But I didn't frown
My crotch was stirring
Anticipating to be released
A breeze took to her hair
Then she started to cease
She sat up on me
I was manipulating her breasts
Loving her view
A precious treasure chest

SHE UNZIPS MY MEMBER
SOLID AS CONCRETE
ACHING TO BE TOUCHED
SUDDENLY HER LIPS GREET
MY HEART RACES
UP AND DOWN SHE GOES
TICKLING HER NIPPLES
MORE AND MORE SHE BLOWS
I TOLD HER PLEASE
SHE LOOKED AT ME IN HALF PACE
I TOLD HER I'M HUNGRY
PLEASE SIT ON MY FACE
SHE LOWERED HER PANTIES
HER LIPS START TO SWELL
HER HIPS LOWER TO MY FACE
MY ANXIETY COMPELS
HER LIPS ENGORGE MINE
AS SHE GRINDS AWAY
RIDING MY FACE
LIKE RUDOLPH ON SANTA'S SLEIGH
SHE MOANED OUT LOUD
SHE QUIVERED
MY TONGUE WAS PLAYING PIN BALL
PLEASURE WAS DELIVERED
SHE HAD TO MOVE
SHE COULDN'T TAKE IT ANY MORE
HER BODY WAS ACHING
SHE WANTED AN ORGASM TO HER CORE
I CLIMBED ON TOP OF HER
I WAS IN THE DRIVER'S SEAT
I SANK ALL THE WAY IN

PLEASANTLY COMPLETE
PLEASURE ERUPTED
MOANS WERE MANY
I GAVE HER THE PASSION
SHE SAID IT WAS PLENTY
HER BODY GUSHED
MINE EXPLODED TOO
WE WERE STUCK AS ONE
COMPLETELY IN LOVE GLUE
THE HOOD OF HER CAR
IT WENT FOR A JOY RIDE
CREAMY PASSION
YET BONA-FIDE

Her Beautiful Breasts

Her beautiful breasts
They stared right at me
My jar dropped in awe
Beautiful, like grapes hanging in a vineyard
Soft and supple
It brought moisture to my mouth
Salivating at the depth of these angelic beauties
I walked towards them
I cupped them in my hand
My kisses landed on this beautiful flesh
Every inch a kiss was made
Her nipples were erect
My tongue glided over them
They were complete with my saliva
Her beautiful breasts were saturated
Saturated with all my love
Stained with my nutrients of lust

WE CAME TOGETHER

OUR FEELINGS EMERGED
OUR DESIRES WERE BURNING
AN INFATUATION AT ITS PEAK
WE WERE NEVER PHYSICALLY CLOSE
THE WORDS WE SHARED HEIGHTENED OUR AROUSAL
STIMULATION OCCURRED BETWEEN US
MOANS OF PLEASURE WERE HUNDREDS OF MILES AWAY
HEAT WAS RISING FROM OUR BODIES
OUR CLOSENESS WAS COMING TOGETHER
OUR HEARTS WERE RACING
BODIES SHAKING
IT WAS EXPLOSIVE AND BREATH TAKING
WE LAID THERE IN A COMA
PLEASURED BY OUR WORDS
FILTHY DIRTY THOUGHTS RELEASED FROM OUR BODIES
COMPLETELY EXHAUSTED
WE CAME TOGETHER

HOTEL HALLWAY

THERE SHE WAS
STANDING THERE IN THE HALLWAY
OUR EYES GRAZED EACH OTHER'S PRESENCE
I WALKED TO MY ROOM BUT COULDN'T LOOK AWAY
I SLIPPED MY KEY IN THE DOOR
THE DOOR SWUNG OPEN BUT IT DIDN'T CLOSE
I LOOKED BEHIND ME
AND PERFUME WENT UP MY NOSE
THAT WOMAN WAS IN MY DOORWAY
WALKING STRAIGHT TO ME
A LITTLE BIT ALARMED
BUT I COULDN'T FLEE
SHE GRABBED MY FACE
HER HEAD TURNED
HER TONGUE WAS DOWN MY THROAT
PASSION WAS QUICKLY LEARNED
SHE PUSHED ME BACKWARDS
TO THE BED I FELL
A NERVOUS WRECK
MY PANTS STARTED TO SWELL
WE STARTED RIPPING AT OUR CLOTHES
HOLES STARTED TO FORM
HER SKIN TOUCHED MINE
SHE WAS SOFT AND WARM
SHE KISSED ME MORE
MY TOWER WAS FULL OF CEMENT
SHE GRAZED IT WITH HER TONGUE AND
DOWN HER THROAT IT WENT

I MOANED OUT LOUD
IT WAS HARD TO BEAR
WATCHING HER ENJOY
MY LOVE STICK DOWN THERE
SHE LOWERED HER PANTIES
HER TACO WAS WET
LOVE MAKING WAS STANDING BY
OUR TOOLS CAME TOGETHER AND MET
SIGHS OF PLEASURE
OF THIS JOYFUL TIME
SWEET JUICES FLOWING
CITRUS LIME
HER BREASTS BOUNCED
I SUCKED HER NIPS
GRINDING OUR MEATS
SWAYING AT OUR HIPS
OUR BODIES DRUNK
DESTINY WAS ON THE RISE
ORGASMS COMING
IT'S SHOWN IN OUR EYES
PASSIONATE SOUNDS EMERGE
SWEAT RUSHES LIKE THE SHORE
OUR LOVE MIXES
OUR JUICE STARTS TO POUR

MATH TUTOR

I STRUGGLED IN SCHOOL
ESPECIALLY WITH MATH
I ALWAYS TRIED MY BEST
IT WAS A DIFFICULT PATH
I WAITED IN MY CLASSROOM
FOR MY TUTOR TO ARRIVE
WORRIED ABOUT FAILING
LOOKING AT THE CLOCK THAT WAS AFTER FIVE
HIGH HEELS WHERE CLACKING
MY HEART RACED
SHE OPENED THE DOOR
MY JAW DROPPED MY FACE
HER BLACK FLOWING HAIR
WALKING TO ME
HER BREASTS BOUNCING OUT
TRYING TO BREAK FREE
I STUTTERED OVER MY WORDS
MY PALMS WERE WET
SHE WAS SLEEK AS A MODEL
MY HEART RACED LIKE A JET
I OPENED MY BAG
TOOK OUT MY BOOK
SHE SAT NEXT TO ME
I WAS AMAZED AT HOW SHE LOOKED
SHE SAW ME STARING
AT HER BEAUTIFUL BREASTS
MY HEART WAS IN TROUBLE
BEATING FROM MY CHEST

HER EYES LOOKED ME OVER
A SULTRY VIXEN SHE WAS
I COULD NOT FOCUS
JUST LOOKING AT HER GAVE ME A BUZZ
I DIDN'T UNDERSTAND WHAT SHE WAS TEACHING
MY MIND WAS GONE
THINKING HOW DELICIOUS SHE MIGHT TASTE
MUNCHING ON HER LAWN
SHE SAW ME NOT PAYING ATTENTION
SHE GRABBED MY HAND
I STOOD UP SHAKING
SHE HAD SOMETHING PLANNED
SHE WHISKED ME AWAY
ACTING LIKE THE BOSS
DROOLING OVER HER ASS
IN MY MIND I WANTED TO TOSS
ANOTHER DOOR OPENED
SHE SAT ME IN THE CHAIR
SHE CLOSED THE DOOR
NOW HER BREASTS WERE BARE
MY MANHOOD JOLTED
IT STOOD AT ATTENTION
DID I DO SOMETHING WRONG?
DO I HAVE DETENTION?
SHE TOLD ME TO STAND
I DID WHAT SHE SAID
MY PANTS CAME DOWN
HER LIPS TOUCHED MY HEAD
I FONDLED HER BREASTS
SO SMOOTH AND RIPE
I RUBBED HER CLIT

JUST BELOW HER RACING STRIPE
MY BODY STARTED TO SHAKE
AN INTERNAL EARTHQUAKE
VANILLA SPILLED OUT
DOWN HER THROAT WENT MY MILKSHAKE
I LAY ON THE FLOOR
AS SHE SUCKED HER THUMB
I DIDN'T CARE AT ALL
THAT IN MATH I WAS STILL DUMB
THE ROOM WAS FULL OF DESIRE
EVERYTHING CONTINUED TO SPIN
SHE OPENED THE DOOR
SHE LEFT ME WITH A GRIN

My Waitress

Good evening miss
What is good on this menu?
I love something soft and chewy
Could that be you?
What beverages are good?
I want what's the best
I want desert too
Can I eat that off your chest?
What else do you have?
I want something good to taste
Can I just bite your lips?
They are so desirable to trace
Do you have anything soft?
Maybe something I could squeeze?
Like some beautiful dough
Or maybe your precious butt please
Do you have any sample kisses?
I hope you came prepared
Looking into your sweet Indian eyes
I'm telling you, I'm not scared
I will be waiting for my food
I hope you prepare it with a dirty mind
You sexy vixen
I love your soft behind
Stop teasing me
My pants are bulging out
Feed me beautiful
Your tasty love is what I'm about

She Awaits Me

I take this ladder
I climb up to your lair
I see the candles bouncing
I see you in the candle glare
You're covered in satin
Your hair is flowing from the wind
I step inside
Already I have sinned
I look at you deeply
I bite my bottom lip
You slip off your gown
Exposing your beautiful nips
I start to drool
At your angelic sight
My palms start sweating
My body is getting tight
You walk towards me
Like a cat on the prowl
Your lips touch mine
Internally I howl
We sway back and forth
As the window lets in a breeze
You whisper in my ear
"You are what I want to please"
Your tongue plays with mine
My hands roam your chest
My belt is being removed
My body is full of zest

YOU THROW ME DOWN
I LAND ON THE BED
ALL MY CLOTHES ARE TORN
A RAZOR BLADE LIKE SHRED
YOU CRAWL ON TOP OF ME
HOVERING OVER MY TOWER
YOU SAID, "THIS IS MINE"
IT'S NOW TIME TO DEVOUR
SLOWLY YOU SIT DOWN
EMERGING OUR SAUCE
YOU START RIDING ME
LIKE YOU ARE MY BOSS
WE SLIP AND SLIDE
IN THE VALLEY OF YOUR FLOWER
YOU MOAN MY NAME
YOU HAVE ALL THE POWER
OUR BODIES TREMBLE
AN EARTHQUAKE IS ABOUT TO SHAKE
PULSES THROBBING
WE LAY THERE COVERED IN OUR PASSIONATE LAKE!

TASTING YOU

I JUST WANT TO EAT YOU LIKE A VULTURE
PEELING BACK THE LAYERS OF YOUR SKIN
I WANT TO TASTE THE CITRUS OF YOUR BODY
MAKING IMPRESSIONS WITH MY LIPS
I WANT TO MAKE YOUR CONTOURS EMERGE IN GOOSE
BUMPS
I WANT TO HEAR YOUR MOANS AS I CLENCH DOWN MY
TEETH ON YOUR SUPPLE SKIN
I HOPE YOU REMEMBER ME FOREVER
YOUR BODY WILL BE CALLING ME BACK
I WANT MY SALIVA STAINS TO SATURATE YOUR SOUL
I WANT TO CLAIM YOU WITH MY TONGUE
LET THE POETRY OF MY TONGUE GUIDE YOU TO THE
NECTAR I CAME SEARCHING FOR
I LEAVE YOU TONIGHT
SATURATED
IN YOUR OWN BLISS!!!

GOOD EVENING BEAUTIFUL

DON'T YOU LOOK CUTE?
IN THOSE BLACK LACED PANTIES
DO YOU MIND IF I JOIN YOU?
TO FULFILL ALL OF MY FANTASIES
LET ME START
I WANT TO PLAY A DOMINANT ROLL
I WANT YOUR MIND TO SUBMIT
MY THOUGHTS ARE OUT OF CONTROL
I'VE BEEN THINKING DIRTY
THROUGHOUT MY DAY
CAN I TASTE YOUR FINGER?
BECAUSE I SAW YOU STARTING TO PLAY
BUT WAIT SWEETIE
DON'T YOU NEED MY TONGUE?
YOUR LIPS LOOK SWOLLEN
WHAT HAVE YOU DONE?
YOUR FINGER IS DELICIOUS
ALL YOUR MILKY FLOW
LICKING MY LIPS
MMMM, TO MY TUMMY IT GOES
YOU'RE FLAVORFUL
JUST AS I THOUGHT
I AM A HANDYMAN
DID YOU SEE THE TOOLS I BROUGHT?
YOU'VE BEEN TURNING ME ON
FOR SO DAMN LONG
MY DICK IS TURNING TO CEMENT
THIS IS JUST SO WRONG

NAKED AND FREE
YOUR KISSES SWARM
I ENTER YOUR MOUTH
SO PRECIOUS AND WARM
MY EYES ROLL
EVERYTHING IS DOWN YOUR THROAT
RAMMING YOUR FACE
MOANING SOUNDS LIKE A BILLY GOAT
YOU COME UP FOR AIR
YOU WANT ME INSIDE YOUR FLOWER
PASSION BURNING OUR DESIRES
ECSTASY FILLS THE ROOM FOR MORE THAN AN HOUR

Hot Tub Bliss

Good evening sweetie
I guess you got my note
Join me in here
Let's make white caps in this boat
I know this feels weird
Here take this gin
We all live a different life
We all have a little sin
Drop your clothes
I've been day dreaming about you all day
My words are in my kisses
Please join me and let's play
You look smoking hot
You look beautiful under these candles
It's just the perfect light
Enough for our eyes to handle
Your flower looks delicious
I love licking my lips
Naked and sultry
With your rock hard nips
How does that water feel?
I love the bubbles that surround your skin
Will you kiss me?
Or do you want me to begin?
Come closer
My lips are wet
I've been naughty
I'm all set

KISSES START TO MELT
THE HOT TUB BUBBLES MORE
DANCING IN UNITY
STANDING ON THIS WET FLOOR
HANDS ARE ROLLING ACROSS OUR BODIES
STEAM IS EMERGING
SIN IS IN THE AIR
ROMANCE IS SPLURGING
HER HANDS START TO FISH
SHE MEETS UP TO MY SNAKE
IT GROWS IN HER HANDS
MY MIND STARTS TO BAKE
WE WRESTLE TO GAIN CONTROL
NOW IN MY ARMS UPSIDE DOWN
HER MOUTH IS AROUND MY TOWER
AS MY FACE IS IN HER MOUND
SEVERAL SLURPS AND GULPS
TONGUES FLY
A SEXY EVENING
IN A STARLIT SKY
THE AROUSAL HEIGHTENS
I PLACE HER BACK IN THE TUB
BACK IN THE WATER
SHE LOWERS ON MY STUB
PLEASURE SOUNDS POUR FROM OUR MOUTHS
WHITE WATER IS THRASHING
OUR UNITS IN FULL FORCE
UP AND DOWN SMASHING
HER BREASTS SWING IN MY FACE
I BOB FOR HER GLOBES
MY FINGER REACHES AROUND BACK

HER BUTT WASN'T CLOSED
ECSTASY FORMED
SIGHS OF PLEASURE
DEEP INSIDE HER
PLENTY TO MEASURE
OUR EYES ROLL
OUR BONES GET TIGHT
ORGASMS SHOOT BETWEEN US
IN THIS HOT TUB DELIGHT
OHHHHH SWEETHEART
THAT WAS A FOREVER SIN
I LOVE YOU AS MY SECRETARY
YOU BETTER GET GOING TO YOUR HUSBAND

Making Love To Your Breasts

I just want to make love to your breasts
Feeling your softness between my tower
Slowly gliding back and forth
Into mind blowing pleasures
Watching you hold your soft clouds
As my manhood peeks out at your chin
The sweet sounds of love awakening on each
stroke
My eyes roll as you grin
Pumping faster and faster
Biting at your lips
As our frictions collide
Your nipples standing at attention
As I pause to clamp my lips around them
Moans scatter the candle lit room
Finding my way back between your mountains
Arousal is beginning overcome me
Tingling mounting from this smooth glide
Our bodies stir
Wrestling with our desires
Eruption overloads your chest
As it slowly seeps into your pores
Wiping the excess of love on your divine skin

In The Bedroom

We stared at each other
Naked in awe
Delivering messages with our eyes
From the burning passion we saw
I took her in my arms
I threw her on the bed
I started eating her pussy
While she bobbed and gave me head
We were stacked neatly
We were seventy minus one
Licking and slurping
Moaning just begun
Our stomachs rose
Our breathes became deep
Cloudy minds
Our genitals started to seep
Tasting our love
Passion filled our lips
Our bodies connected
Grinding at our hips
My tongue poked deeper into her folds
As she let out a deep sighhhh
Her body stood like a cobra
And howled to the sky
My rod between her palms
At the stroke of midnight
My eyes roll
With a passionate delight

OUR BODIES GET WEAKER
EXPLOSIONS ARE CHURNING
STEAM FROM OUR BODIES
DESIRES ARE BURNING
THE PEAK IS NEAR
OUR ORGANS HAVE BEEN FED
COMING IS THE GRAND FINALE
MOMENTARILY ON THIS BED
ORGASM IS NEARING
AROUSAL IS AT ITS PEAK
COME POURED FROM BOTH OF US
MINE EXPLODED OFF HER CHEEKS
DRIPPING MOUTHS
GLOSSY WITH A SHIMMER
EATING OUR DELICIOUS FLESH
IT'S HOW WE ENJOY OUR DINNER

On My Grand Piano

The room was filled with bouncing candles
I sat down at my grand piano
My girlfriend arrived and joined me
A bottle of wine popped open
Two glasses were poured
She sat on top of the piano
Her red dress flowing from the ceiling fans
I start to play
Melodies ran through the air
I watched her drink her wine
As she gets more and more relaxed
She makes eyes at me
The piano is moving her body in erotic ways
She leans over to kiss me
Her seductive kiss of wine is tasty
I stroke the keys and the music makes her body
dance
The more I play, the room echoes with desire
She starts to touch herself on her arms
Watching me play with passion
I watch the passion build in her eyes
Her hands disappear under her dress
Seeing her stomach rise
She moans at the vibrations under her
She peers into my eyes with a naughty look
Turned on by the sensual music I play
She faces towards me

SHE PULLS UP HER DRESS TO EXPOSE HER FLOWER TO
ME
IT'S WET AND TASTY LOOKING
HER FINGERS GLISTEN AND GLOW
THE MUSIC GETS LOUDER
PULSATING HER BODY
SHAKING FEVERISHLY
SHE SINGS TO HER ORGASM
SQUIRTING ON ME AND THE PIANO
MY FINGERS SLIP ON THE KEYBOARD
MAKING STRANGE MUSIC
I FINISH MY BALLET
THE ROOM IS QUIET
SHE'S EXHAUSTED
SHE LOOKS ME DEEP IN MY EYES
SHE OPENS MY MOUTH WITH HER STICKY FINGERS
I TASTE EACH DIGIT TO PERFECTION
SAVORING THE TASTE
SHE KISSES ME DEEPLY
TASTING THE MUSIC WE CREATED

My Naughty Thoughts

You took my innocence
You turned my mind into a dirty play
I've stained these papers
With words of my ink on display
You filtered all my thoughts
When I'm innocent and brave
My mind won't come clean
Now I just misbehave
You swim within my soul
You make me leak
You arouse my interest
I'm now just a freak
My pants extend out
My rod gets stiff
My words for you are divine
I want to climb on your cliff
I've stained my underwear
My love glue secreted
I exhausted my fantasies
Daily, I become depleted
It's your fault
It's you reading this
Dirty desires stuck in my mind
Can I at least have a fantasy kiss?
It's hard to handle
All your images in my mind
Soap can't clean me
Thoughts of you continue to unwind

I CAN'T BE NORMAL
YOU ARE MY OBSESSION
I'M THE POET WRITING THESE
I THINK I NEED CONFESSION
MY THOUGHTS ABOUT YOU ARE INSANE
I DON'T KNOW WHAT ELSE TO DO
IF YOU WERE IN FRONT OF ME NOW
I WOULD MAKE STEAMY LOVE TO YOU

HER BEEF CURTAINS

SHE LAID THERE ON THE RUFFLED SHEETS
HER BEEF CURTAINS WERE OPEN
LOOKING LIKE A BEAUTIFUL BUTTERFLY
FLAPPING ITS SATURATED WINGS
AWAITING MY TONGUE
I KNEEL DOWN BESIDE HER
KISSING HER SOFT BODY
SHE BEGS ME TO EAT
LICKING MY LIPS
I KISS MY WAY DOWN TO HER INNER THIGHS
PAUSING
A FEW SOFT BLOWS MAKE HER TINY HAIRS DANCE
SOFT AND WET LOOKING
SATURATED BY EXCITEMENT
MY TONGUE FLICKS HER CREAMY FOLDS
HER STOMACH RISES
VOLCANIC ASH ERUPTS FROM HER MOUTH
BLOWING STEAM
HER SKIN PERCOLATES WITH EROTIC PLEASURE
I CLAMP DOWN ON HER LIPS
HUMMING A TUNE
VIBRATING HER INNER THIGHS
SHE ROLLS AROUND LIKE AN ALLIGATOR
CLAMPING DOWN MORE
SWOLLEN AND GLISTENING
HER HIPS HUMP MY FACE
I WATCH HER FACE MAKE CLOWN GESTURES
EYES ROLLING

HAIR PULLING
HER BODY IS SHAKING
MOANS AND SIGHS ERUPT
PASSION LEAKS
MY FACE IS COATED IN LOVE
EXHAUSTED AND DEAD LOOKING
I CLIMB ON TOP OF HER
STARE INTO HER EYES
MY FACE GLISTENS LIKE A ZOMBIE
I KISS HER DEEPLY
THANKING HER FOR DESSERT!

Edible

There she was
Just lying on my bed
Her soft naked curves caressing the bed sheets
My stomach growled
My body was famished just looking at her
She looked so edible
I walked closer to smell her sexy scent
I touched her supple skin
Her arousal was tender
My lips surrounded her nipples
Kissing her breasts with wandering hands
She sighed from my tingling touch
I watched her sink deeper into the bed
Drunk off my sweet soft kisses
Sweet love nectar seeped from her flower
My fingers explored her escape
I sucked my finger with her vanilla on it
Her hips were gyrating
Moaning for me
She rips off my button shirt like a lion
Feeding her soft lips on my neck
My tower still caged and roaring in my pants
Her lips surround my nipples
Tugging gently
I grab her face
I send my tongue down her throat
Our tongues explore our naughty mouths
Enjoying the taste of our passion

SHE PUSHES ME BACKWARDS ON THE BED
CRAWLING TO ME
I SUBMIT TO HER DESIRES
SHE CLIMBS ON TOP OF ME
LOWERING HER WET LIPS TO MY TONGUE
SHE SITS DOWN
I'M SUBMERGED IN HER LOVE
MY TONGUE DANCES INSIDE HER SOFT SKIN FOLDS
SHE MOANS GRABBING AT HER BOUNCY BREASTS
SHE GRINDS ON MY FACE LIKE A MEAT SLICER
SLURPS OF PASSION INSTILL THE AIR
HER STOMACH ROLLS LIKE A TIDE
HER MOANS GET LOUDER
PULLING AT HER HAIR
SHE LEANS BACKWARDS
HER MOUTH OPENS
SHE SCREAAAAAAMMMMMMSSSSS
YES! YES! YES!
HER RIVER OF PASSION FLOWS INSIDE MY MOUTH
SHE FALLS TO THE SIDE EXHAUSTED
I SWALLOW HER SWEET ESSENCE
I CRAWL TO HER AND KISS HER DEEPLY
MY MOUTH SILKY AND WET
SHE WAS DELICIOUS
PRECIOUS AND EDIBLE!

BUBBLE BATH GIGGLES

I FINALLY MADE IT HOME
TO SEE CANDLES BOUNCING OFF THE WALLS
BEAUTIFUL SMELLS IN MY HOME
STRANGE SOUNDS OF CAT CALLS
ROSE PETALS COVERED THE GROUND
IN STRAIGHT LINES TO THE BATHROOM DOOR
I HEARD MORE GIGGLING
PUZZLED, I HAD TO INVESTIGATE MORE
I WALKED SLOWLY TO THE BATHROOM
WHERE TWO VOICES PLAYED
MY GIRLFRIEND AND OUR NEIGHBOR
IN THE HOT TUB NAKED ON DISPLAY
I WATCHED AT THE DOORWAY
EYEING MY NEIGHBOR JESS
SHE WOULD ALWAYS JOG WAVING AT ME
BOUNCING HER BEAUTIFUL BREASTS
MESMERIZED, I WATCHED THEM GIGGLE
I EVEN SAW A PLAYFUL KISS
MY HEART WAS POUNDING
NOT ANOTHER MOMENT I COULD MISS
I ENTERED THE DOORWAY
JESS AND MY GIRLFRIEND STARED ME DOWN
I FELT SO NERVOUS
MY HEART STARTED TO POUND
TO THEM, IT SEEMED ORDINARY
LIKE I'M SUPPOSED TO SEE THEIR NAKED BREASTS
BUT MY EYES WERE FIXATED
ON THEIR SEXY CHESTS

I LEANED OVER THE TUB TO KISS MY BABE
JESS STOOD UP WITH HER SOAPY TITS
SCAVENGING FOR MY CROTCH
MY COCK TURNED TO A ROCK WITH HER SOAPY MITS
MY GIRLFRIEND WINKED
LIKE THIS WAS PLANNED
I MELTED LIKE BUTTER
I BARELY COULD STAND
JESS TOOK DOWN MY ZIPPER
MY GIRLFRIEND TOOK OUT MY SNAKE
BOTH OF THEIR HANDS WERE ON ME
MY VOICE IS STARTING TO BREAK
MY PANTS GET LOWERED
AS THEY SAT UP ON THEIR KNEES
LOOKING DEEPLY IN MY EYES
LIKE PUPPY DOGS SAYING PLEASE
THEY ATTACKED ME FROM EACH SIDE OF THE BASE
LICKING UP AND DOWN LIKE A TYPEWRITER
MY EYES ROLL BACK IN MY HEAD
I'M TRYING TO BE A FIGHTER
THEIR LIPS MAKE MY SKIN SILKY SMOOTH
JESS TAKES ME DOWN HER THROAT
MY GIRLFRIEND KISSES MY BALLS
I WAS STRUGGLING TO COPE
MY GIRLFRIEND TAKES HER TURN
SWAPPING MOUTHS
MY HANDS DO SOME WANDERING
AT THEIR SOAPY CHESTS DOWN SOUTH
MY MIND IS STARTING TO GET DRUNK
MY BODY IS STARTING TO SHAKE
AN EARTH QUAKE IS STIRRING IN MY BALLS

TWO BEAUTIFUL WOMEN ON MY SNAKE
I BOUNCE JESS'S DOUBLE D'S
BUBBLES FORM IN THE AIR
MY GRIMACING FACE EMERGES
HOW MUCH THESE BEAUTIES CARE
THEY BOTH MAKE OUT IN FRONT OF ME
MY TOWER IS ACTING LIKE THE MIC
MY INTERNAL GEARS ARE ROLLING
MY EYES SEE WHAT THEY LIKE
MY GIRLFRIEND DEEP THROATS ME TO THE BASE
JESS LICKS HER LIPS
PULLING AT MY TIE
TOUCHING AT HER SENSUAL HIPS
MY BODY IS NEAR THE BREAKING POINT
WHERE MY LOVE IS STARTING TO SOB
THEY ARE EATING ME SIDE BY SIDE
LIKE I'M A PIECE OF CORN ON THE COB
MY MOANS GET DEEP
I PULL THEIR FACES AWAY
STROKING MY TOWER LIKE A MACHINE GUN
I START TO SPRAY
LOADS OF LOVE FLIES
DRIPPING ON TO THEIR BEAUTIFUL FACES
DRIPPING DOWN THEIR NECKS
IN THEIR SWEET SOFT SPACES
I COLLAPSE OVER THE EDGE OF THE TUB
KISSES START TO POUR
WE ALL START MAKING OUT TOGETHER
ALL THREE TONGUES DANCE FOR A SALTY DANCE ONCE
MORE

SHE WAS MY POEM

SHE WAS MY POEM
I GENTLY LAID HER DOWN ON MY BED
HER NAKED BODY GLISTENED
EVERY CONTOUR OF HER SKIN WAS EXPOSED
SHE LOOKED DELICIOUS
MOUTH WATERING
A TEMPTRESS QUEEN
THE PEN WAS MY TONGUE
I OUTLINED MY LOVE AROUND HER SKIN
MY SALIVA WAS THE INK OF THIS PRECIOUS POEM
HER CURVES ALLOWED ME TO WRITE MORE
FEELINGS POURED FROM MY MOUTH
EXPLORING ALL OVER HER CANVAS
HER TINY BODY HAIRS APPLAUDED
HEIGHTENED BY THE DROPS OF MY INK
HER SILKY SKIN WAS MOIST FROM THE POETRY
WRITTEN
THE DESIRES KEPT BURNING
TONGUE FLICKS GLIDING ON HER CARAMEL SKIN
SHE WAS ADORABLE LOOKING
PANTING AND SQUIRMING
DESIRED BY THE NIGHTS LUST
MY POETRY WAS WRITTEN
WITH MY TONGUE
SHE WAS MY NAKED CANVAS
SHE WAS MY POEM

Oh Santa

.....Santa comes down the chimney.....

Hey Santa, how do I look under the mistletoe?
Where is my finger? Where did it go?
I've been dreaming, I've been really bad,
My kids are asleep; it's been awhile since I had!
A big dick!!
I know you are busy but please tame my
naughty ass,
Make me purr, I want to be out of gas.
Come to the kitchen, I have cookies and egg nog,
Undo your belt and take out your fat log!
Ho ho ho ho hooooo!
Mmmmm, Santa, your desire is a must,
How do you like my teddy and my bust?
Touch me Santa; I want the feel of Saint Nick,
Your red pants are growing, I want your dick!
Take my clothes off under this mistletoe,
I want you balls deep, please don't go slow.
Mmmm, stuff my stocking you jolly fat man,
How does my ass look? Please grab my tits if
you can!
Pound me Santa; stuff me with your cream,
I've waited forever for this wet dream.
Mmmm Santa, you know how to pound my taco,
Let me ride you, like a bronco.
Roll over big boy,
Stuff in your meaty toy!

How do you like my big tits?
Take off your white gloves and use your mits.
You better not tell Mrs. Claus,
That my body was ravaged by your filthy paws.
Oh Santa, are you getting ready to cum?
Do you like me sucking my thumb?
Ohhhhh ho ho ho,
Santa did you go?
Mmmm Santa, thank you for coming in me,
My pussy is vibrating like a bumble bee.
Exhausted by the release,
Bodies cease!
Hey Santa! Make sure you get carrots for your reindeer,
So they can have some energy for the flight dear!
Mommy mommy! Where are you?
Holy shit Santa, what am I going to do?
Hey kids, I'll be up in a minute or two!
Santa! You must go,
Down the hallway Santa went, ho ho ho!

So You Want To Flirt

So you want to flirt?
By the end of the night, we will roll in some dirt.
Go ahead; take off your bra and shirt,
Lie on your bed and pull down your skirt.
Touch your breasts, lifting them from north to south,
Close your eyes and imagine my tender mouth.
I'll start on your neck,
Wait! Mmm just a peck.
I want to watch your skin rise,
So I can devour you with my seductive surprise.
Think of me lowering my tongue,
Flicking your nipples, oh so fun!
I love watching your body shiver,
From the prowl of my tongue I deliver.
You try squirming from my mount,
Thousands of kisses I count.
Your body gets restless and starts to purr,
Grabbing at my hair quite secure.
Soft kisses land on your inner thighs,
Watching your face, looking at your eyes.
As they roll back inside your head,
My tongue slithers to the moisture on this bed.
Your flower starts to leak,
Rolling to the folds of your butt cheeks.
I capture the runaway leak,
As your moans start to shriek.

BITING, NIBBLING MAKING EVERYTHING WET,
FISTS FULL OF HAIR WITH MY FACE IN YOUR NET.
TONGUE FLICKS IN YOUR VENUS FLY TRAP,
SLAP, SLAP, SLAP!
AS YOUR BACK ARCHES LIKE A BRIDGE,
MY MOUTH IS WET LIKE A ZOMBIE, MORE THAN A
SMIDGE.
OCEANS POUR,
MORE! MORE! MORE!
UHHHHGGGGG!
YOUR BODY STARTS TO CEASE,
PULLING MY HEAD AWAY, SAYING THANK YOU, **TEASE!**

Your Hostage

I just want to be your hostage
Tell me anything you want
My desires burn for you
I just love the way your body flaunts

I've been in the closet far too long
It's time to unleash my devilish side
I'm shaking within my bones
I'm not going to hide

I'm seeking pleasure
I want to be your vice
Your sultry vixen body on mine
Please let's roll the dice

My body is your canvas
Do with it as you please
Just let me nibble at you
When you come closer on your knees

I'm squirming in these ropes
I want your beautiful landscape
Your breasts are driving me wild
Place them in my face so they don't escape

Please, I can't take to much more
I need you right now
My devilish grin protrudes

MY TEETH ARE READY TO SINK IN AND PLOW
MY BLOOD IS BOILING
I NEED YOU SO MUCH
ECSTASY IS BREWING
YOU'RE TOO FAR FOR ME TO TOUCH

JUST SLIDE YOUR SKIN ON MINE
SO I COULD LICK YOUR FLESH
SO I CAN TASTE YOUR SKIN
BITE OFF YOUR PANTIES THAT ARE MESH

YOU'VE TEASED ME FOR TOO LONG
PLEASE FUCK MY BRAINS OUT
YOU'VE SEEN MY DESIRE GROW
MY LIPS CONTINUE TO POUT

UNLOCK MY HANDS
YOU ARE GOING TO BE MY THANKSGIVING MEAL
EVERY INCH OF YOUR BODY
MY TONGUE IS GOING TO STEAL

DRAIN

DRAIN
INTO ME
YOUR NAUGHTY THOUGHTS
MAKE ME WHIMPER
MAKE ME LEAK
DANCE YOUR EMOTIONS
ON ME
PLAY WITH MY ENVISIONS
MAKE ME REMEMBER
EVERY DETAIL
TAME ME
DEVOUR MY BODY
I WANT TO BE YOUR EDIBLE DESIRE
STAIN MY SKIN
MARK YOUR TERRITORY
THRUST INTO MY DREAMS

HER NAKED CANVAS

HER NAKED CANVAS SITS BEFORE ME
MY EYES ARE WIDE OPEN
PUZZLED BY HER BEAUTY
MY MIND TURNING ITS GEARS
WONDERING WHERE I CAN KISS FIRST
WONDERING WHERE I CAN STAIN HER WITH MY SALIVA
WONDERING WHAT PART I CAN SINK MY TEETH INTO
I SALIVATE MORE
MY FINGERS STIR
SHE IS LIKE A THANKSGIVING MEAL BEFORE ME
LICKING MY LIPS
DEVOURING HER INSIDE MY MIND
WANTING TO TASTE EVERY BIT OF HER FLESH
DREAMING OF A MOMENT LIKE THIS
DESIRING THIS POEM TO COME TO LIFE
IT HURTS
BECAUSE I'M LOOKING AT HER PICTURE

BAY WINDOW

She stood there
At her bay window
Gazing at the moon
With the breeze
Draping across her skin
Thinking about her past
How she dreams of love
With a deep sigh
She walks away
Lighting several candles in her room
The glow dancing off the walls
While the breeze
Whispers through her window
Standing in front of her bed
Undoing her top
Her breasts exposed to the moonlight
Closing her eyes and twirling her hair
Deeply remembering her past
Lowering her panties
Walking to her window again
Her cherry nipples rise
With her skin caressed by the moon
Slowly turning away to her bed
She sinks into her plush mattress
Barricading her naked body in her satin sheets
Delicate softness on her skin
She becomes flushed with desire

Softly roaming her hands on her voluptuous
breasts
Fingers tickling and pinching her nipples
Her body temperature rises
Gliding her finger tips along her inner thighs
Her soft delicious curves understanding her
touch
Deep sighs release from her mouth
Touching her skin folds
Moisture seeps on her glistening fingers
Sinking deeper as her other hand rakes her
inner thighs
Soft pleasurable noises bounce off her walls
Offering beautiful moments in the candle glare
Her chest rises
Her eyes flush
Breathing gets heavier
Her fingers soaked from memories inside her
Her legs shake
Trembling as her toes wiggle
Tightening of her muscles
Contracting jolts of pleasure erupt
Panting
Panting
Panting
A sheen sweat glistens off her soft skin
Rubbing her wet fingers along her breasts
Softly twirling her hair
She looks around
Motionless
To memories of her past

TAKE ME TO YOUR BED

TAKE ME TO YOUR BED
I DON'T CARE ABOUT SIN
WHERE LOVE NEVER MEETS ME HERE
DO WHAT YOU WANT TO BEGIN

TAKE ME TO NEW HEIGHTS
RIP MY CLOTHES FOR ALL I CARE
TOUCH ME ALL OVER
HANDS ARE NEVER THERE

BITE ME EVERYWHERE
DRAW BLOOD IF YOU CAN
I WANT YOU TO CONSUME ME
THIS WAS REALLY NEVER MY PLAN

I JUST NEED SOMEONE TO LOVE ME
I DON'T GET THIS IN MY HOME
PORNOGRAPHY IS MY ONLY LOVER
I'M SO TIRED OF BEING ALONE

MAKE ME SCREAM
SMACK MY PALE SKIN
MAKE MY HEART POUND
I REALLY WANT TO GRIN

MAKE YOUR MARKS ON ME
I WANT BRUISES TO SHOW
SO WHEN I GET TO MY HOME

MY SIGNIFICANT OTHER WILL KNOW

I CAN'T BEAR THIS FUCKING PAIN
I'M TIRED OF BEING TRASH
MAKE MY BODY YOURS
I ALREADY FEEL DEAD AND BURNED TO ASH

I FEEL LIKE A CACTUS
IN A DESERT OF EMPTINESS
PLEASE MAKE ME REMEMBER THIS
MY BEAUTIFUL BLACK HAIRED RAVEN PRINCESS

BURN ME WITH A CANDLE
WHIP ME IF YOU COULD
PLEASE TATTOO YOUR SCENT ON ME
GIVE IT TO ME GOOD

MAKE ME CUM
I WANT TO EXPLODE ON YOUR SKIN
WIPING MY LOVE ON YOU
LET'S PLAY REPEAT AGAIN

I KNOW I WILL DIE A LONELY MAN
SO MUCH LOVE I HAVE ALREADY MISSED
CAN I STAY HERE FOREVER?
TO MAKE LOVE OFTEN AND BE KISSED

At The Front Door

There she stood
In a silky white gown
At the threshold of her door
I approach slowly
Noticing her see through teddy
Nervousness thumped in my heart
Greetings ignite
As I stare into her eyes
I slowly walk into candles glowing
My heart raced
The door closes and two locks click
My back was turned looking into the fire place
Footsteps came behind me
I turn around
Looking into her beautiful eyes
I didn't know if she was Italian or Indian
Sultry black hair down to her lower back
She winked
Grabbing my face to move towards hers
Her soft lips touched mine
Her tongue was flavorful of cinnamon
Our lips were being stretched and pulled
My neck started to get attacked by her teeth
I submitted to her sins
Fantasizing about this day
My buttoned shirt got ruffled
Buttons began to fly
My chest became exposed

HER TONGUE FOUND MY NIPPLES
SAYING HELLO TO HER WET MOUTH
MY EYES ROLLED
MY MUSCLES TIGHTEN
SHE GRIPPED MY SHAFT THAT STARTED GROWING
HER FINGERS FUMBLED FOR MY ZIPPER
MY BREATHES HEIGHTENED
MY PANTS HIT THE FLOOR
SHE LOOKED UP AT ME WITH HER GOTHIC EYES
MY SHAFT DISAPPEARED DOWN HER TENDER THROAT
AS I TRY AND WATCH THE ILLUMINATION AGAINST THE
GLOW OF CANDLES
MY LEGS SHOOK
HER TONGUE FLIPPED AROUND
I LIFTED HER UP TO KISS ME
PUSHING HER TOWARDS THE COUCH
RIPPING AT HER TEDDY
HER BREASTS CAME EXPOSED
MY HANDS BEGAN TO EXPLORE HER SOFTNESS
HER ERECT NIPPLES MET MY LIPS
SUCKING SLOWLY
WATCHING HER HEAD THRASH AROUND
I KISSED HER DEEPLY
PUSHING HER ON THE COUCH
I GRABBED HER LEG AND BITE AT HER INNER THIGHS
SHE MOANED
DROPPING TO THE FLOOR LIKE A HUNGRY WOLF
MY TEETH SNARL
I WATCH HER ANTICIPATION
AS SHE SUBMITS TO ME

I PAUSE
LOOKING INTO HER EYES
MY TEETH CLENCHING DOWN ON HER LACE THONG
RIPPING AT THE EDGES
THEY SNAP
AS I CHEWED THE STRINGS IN MY MOUTH
I LICKED MY LIPS AT HER BEAUTIFUL DAMP MOUND
SLOWLY PARTING THEM
NIBBLING LIKE A VULTURE ON ROAD KILL
HER MOANS FILLED THE AIR
SLURPING HER LOVE
AS SHE GRABBED MY HAIR
HER EYES FLUSH
FLICKING AT HER OPEN BUTTERFLY WINGS
SOBBING AT MY SEDUCTIVE TONGUE
SHE TELLS ME TO **STOP!!!**
PULLING MY FACE TOWARDS HER
SHE TASTES MY SILKY TONGUE
AS WE STAND
STOKING MY WAND IN HER HAND
THROWING ME BACK TOWARDS THE COUCH
STRADDLING ME
CLAIMING ME AS HERS
I ENTER HER
GRABBING AT HER DANGLING BREASTS
THRASHING IN MY FACE
LICKING HER NIPPLES AS THEY SMEAR MY FACE
UP AND DOWN
SWEAT GLISTENING
VEINS MAXED OUT
HER KISSES FLOWING ON MY FACE

EXCITEMENT IS PEAKING
HEARTS RACING
OUR EYES ROLL
GASPING FOR AIR
OUR LOVE UNITED
SQUIRTING JUICES FLOW
COLLAPSING OUR BODIES
DEAD
COMPLETE
PARALYZED
UNITED
REFRESHED
WE LAID THERE BREATHING DEEPLY
WATCHING THE FIRE
WATCHING THE CANDLES GLOW
OUR SPEECH WAS SLURRED
OUR BRAINS WERE FUCKED
OUR BODIES LAY LIFELESS
WE HELD EACH OTHER
STROKING OUR SLIPPERY SKIN

LADDER TO MY WINDOW

THERE IS A LADDER OUTSIDE
PLEASE BE AS QUIET AS YOU CAN
YOU WILL HEAR MY WHIMPERING SOUNDS
LONELINESS IS MY ORCHESTRA NIGHTLY
CLIMB TO THE SECOND FLOOR
PLEASE JUST TAKE ME AWAY
TAKE ME AWAY INTO THE NIGHT OF SIN
I CAN'T BEAR LONELINESS ANYMORE
I'VE BEEN STARVING FOR SOMEONE'S FLESH ON MINE
CARRY ME INTO YOUR ARMS
DON'T SLIP ON MY TEARS
TAKE ME AWAY TO A BEAUTIFUL PLACE
LAY ME DOWN AND MAKE LOVE TO ME
TOUCH ME AND TATTOO MY SKIN WITH YOUR KISSES
I WANT TO KNOW WHAT LOVE FEELS LIKE
I WANT TO KNOW THAT I'M A NEED
PLEASE KEEP ME CLOSE TO YOUR HEART
NURTURE MY BODY AND DO AS YOU PLEASE
LET OUR MOANS MAKE THE MUSIC OF LIFE
LET OUR ORGASM BECOME FIREWORKS
LET OUR PASSION IGNITE
I WANT A MEMORY
I WANT A SMILE
TAKE ME HOME LATER
FOR I MUST BE THERE
QUIETLY PLACE ME BACK IN MY BED
LEAVE ME LIKE YOU NEVER SEEN ME BEFORE
JUST SO I CAN DREAM AWAY

SO I CAN DREAM ABOUT WHAT I'LL NEVER HAVE
UNTIL MY LAST BREATH
OF ANOTHER NIGHT OF BLISS

GYM FLIRT

OH MY!!
THERE SHE IS
ON THE SAME TREADMILL AS USUAL
SHE ALWAYS LOOKS SO DIVINE
WITH HER SEXY GOTHIC LOOKING BLACK HAIR
SHE ALWAYS WINKS AT ME
I WAVE BACK
MY FACE BLUSHES TO AN APPLE
SHE MAKES ME SO SHY
MY EYES ARE MAGNETIC TO HER
WITH HER TIGHT SPANDEX
HER BEAUTIFUL BREASTS BOUNCING LIKE SUCCULENT
GRAPES OFF A VINEYARD VINE
I CAN NEVER FOCUS
WORKING OUT IS VERY DIFFICULT
I SEE HER WATCHING ME
MY SETS BECOME LAZY
I'M JEALOUS OF HER GLISTENING SWEAT
SOAKED BY HER DETERMINATION
OUR EYES SEEM FIXATED ON OUR BODIES
SHOULD I SAY SOMETHING?
I'M SO SCARED
SHE MAKES ME NERVOUS
WE GOT CLOSE AT THE WATER FOUNDATION ONCE
WHILE IN PASSING SHE BIT HER LIP
SHE DRIVES ME INSANE
ARE THESE MIXED MESSAGES?
I NOTICED SHE DOESN'T HAVE A RING

IT'S BEEN MONTHS SEEING HER EYEING ME
AS I DO THE SAME
THE SEXUAL TENSION IS MOUNTING
I'M TOO AFRAID TO SPEAK
EYEING HER AS I GRAB MY BELONGINGS
I WAVE TO HER LIKE A LITTLE KID
AS SHE BLOWS ME A KISS!
GULP!!!

SHE GAVE ME THAT GRIN

SHE GAVE ME THAT GRIN,
MY BODY STARTED CHANGING WITHIN.
WE BOTH KNEW WE WERE ABOUT TO SIN,
BUT KISSES FROM OUR MOUTHS STARTED TO BEGIN.
CLOTHES STARTED FLYING TO THE GROUND,
TWO HEARTS START TO SURGE BLOOD AND POUND.
A LOVING ATTRACTION THAT WE FOUND,
A CANDLE LIT ROOM WITH LOVE MAKING SOUNDS.
IT WAS A DESIRE,
OF PURE DELIGHT FULL OF FIRE.
TWO HEARTS THAT STARTED TO ADMIRE,
UNTIL WE CLIMAX AND THEN RETIRE.
OUR BODIES IN MOTION,
LIKE A THUNDEROUS OCEAN,
LIKE MAGICAL POTION,
FULL OF EXTREME EMOTION.
THE DEED WAS DONE,
WITH LOTS OF FUN,
IT CAN'T BE UNDONE,
BUT WE BOTH WON.

I Want To Bite You

I want to bite you
Into your delicate tender skin
Nibbling on you like road kill
Searching inside your tasty layers
Examining your body with my mouth
Tasting your soft delicious curves
Marking your skin as mine
Tattooing beautiful welts
Giving you wet goose bumps
Watching your heart rise
As I savor your edges
Listening to your soft moans
My buffet
Your skin
My fangs
Your submission
I want to bite you

Last Night Bliss

Last night
She sat on me
We came together
As one
A moment over-do
A time of passion that was needed
We slowly rocked back and forth
Making soft sloshing sounds of love
It was beautiful
Her breasts greeting my lips and tongue
Kisses landed like raindrops
Scattering my love on her
As we exploded together
Glazed over faces
Deep breathing
Glistening skin
A reminder of love
Comatose from passion

I Want To Be

I want to be in her thoughts tonight
As she slowly parts her lips
Letting her fingers glide within her walls
Soaking her fingers in my existence
I want to be on her mind as she moans
Thinking it's me inside her
I want to be the pleasure in each stroke
As she breathes in my soul
I want to be her exhale when she sighs
Breathing in her lust
I want to be the reason she tugs on her erect
Nipples
I want her thoughts to be on me
Flushing out ecstasy
I want her desires to be pleasured by my
Existence
I want her naughtiness to be blamed on me

THE NIGHT JOB

THIS IS MY JOB THAT I HAVE TO DO,
IT'S NOT THE BEST JOB TO BE HAPPY WITH BUT IT
GETS ME THROUGH.
I HAVE TO DO THIS TO FEED MY CHILD,
SOCIAL SERVICES HAVE THREATENED ME AND COURT
PAPERS HAVE BEEN FILED.
I DON'T LIKE WHAT I DO BUT I HAVE NO CHOICE,
I DROPPED OUT OF HIGH SCHOOL AND I HAVE NO
VOICE.
I FEEL TERRIBLE ON HOW I MAKE MY LIVING,
BUT WITH NO EDUCATION NOTHING ELSE IS GIVING.
I STARTED DOING THIS ON MY OWN,
IT'S A TERRIBLE FEELING AND YOU WILL ALWAYS FEEL
ALONE.
PEOPLE ALWAYS SAY THAT SEX SELLS,
BUT SOME DRUGS I USE, I ALWAYS FEEL LIKE I'M IN A
SPELL.
I WISH I COULD DO SOMETHING MORE FULFILLING
OTHER THAN SEX,
BUT LIFE THESE DAYS IS SO HARD AND COMPLEX.
I HAVE NO PIMP OR ANYONE TO WATCH OUT FOR ME,
I HAVE MY OWN EYES TO WATCH AND SEE.
THIS IS ALL I KNOW AND EVERYWHERE I GO,
IT'S SUCH A HARD REALITY IN MY GUT BELOW.
I HAVE BEEN BEATEN AND DEFEATED,
SLEPT WITH MANY HUSBANDS WHO HAVE ALWAYS
CHEATED.

I DON'T DO THIS FOR THE LOVE OR SOME GLORIFIED
BLISS,
IF I COULD FIND A NEW LIFE I WOULD STOP DOING
THIS.
EACH DAY I HAVE TO FIND MORE AND MORE MONEY,
FEEDING MY CLIENTS SEX APPEAL AND MY SWEET
VOICE OF HONEY.
I DO WELL WITH MY USUAL CLIENTS AND MAKE SOME
BIG TIPS,
SOME WANT ME MORE OFTEN MAKING MANY MORE
TRIPS.
SOME MEN REALLY WANT TO WINE AND DINE ME LIKE
I'M SUCH A GEM,
BUT THEY HAVE TO REALIZE THAT I'M NOT INTO THEM.
I'M JUST HERE FOR THE MOMENT TO SUPPORT ME AND
MY CHILD,
WHATEVER I HAVE TO DO FOR MONEY I WILL MAKE
THINGS WILD.
I WILL PERFORM ANYTHING BUT I DO HAVE A LITTLE
PRIDE,
BUT THERE HAVE BEEN A FEW TIMES I'VE REGRETTED
THINGS I'VE TRIED.
WHATEVER IT TAKES TO GET PAID, I WILL PERFORM
THE ACT,
I REALLY CAN'T SAY NO BUT I TRY TO HAVE A LITTLE
TACT.
IT'S USUALLY KIND OF AMUSING SOMETIMES WITH THE
AMOUNT OF MARRIED MEN,
OCCASIONALLY BEING ASKED BY WOMEN EVERY NOW
AND THEN.

I ALWAYS TRY TO BE CAREFUL WITH EVERYTHING I DO,
KEEPING MY EYES ON EVERYTHING IN VIEW.
LUCKILY I HAVE ONLY BEEN HARMED A FEW TIMES,
AFTER A NIGHT OF SEX I TRIED COCAINE LINES.
I REALLY DO MAKE GOOD MONEY AND MOST OF MY CLIENTS DO COME FROM GOOD HOMES,
I GUESS TOO MANY SEXUAL FANTASIES CONTINUE TO ROAM.
THIS IS MY LIFE UNTIL I CAN FIGURE OUT SOMETHING TO CHANGE,
BUT FOR NOW THIS IS HOW MY LIFE WILL ARRANGE.
I REALLY DO LIKE SOME OF THE MEN I HAVE SEX WITH,
THEY TREAT ME WELL AND THEY ALWAYS WANT TO GIVE.
UNFORTUNATELY, THIS IS ONLY A QUICK FLING,
I DON'T THINK MY REPUTATION NOW WOULD MAKE ME CLING.
HOPEFULLY ONE DAY I CAN SEARCH FOR ANOTHER KIND OF JOB,
BUT FOR NOW, MY HEAD WILL CONTINUE TO BOB.

POWDER AND POLES

THE NIGHT STARTS WITH THE MUSIC BOUNCING OFF THE
WALLS,
LISTENING IN THE BACK ROOM TO ALL THE WHISTLING
AND CAT CALLS.
I SIT HERE IN THE CORNER WATCHING THE OTHER
GIRLS SNORT THEIR LINES,
DENTAL FLOSS STRING IN THEIR BUTTS WITH BEAUTIFUL
BEHINDS.
I GET MYSELF READY FOR ANOTHER CRAZY NIGHT,
BUT THE MONEY I RECEIVE IS OUT OF SIGHT.
EYELINER ON AND MASCARA OVER MY EYES,
TRYING TO GET REALLY PRETTY FOR THE BIG SURPRISE.
MY TIME IS SOON TO BE ON THE STAGE,
ENJOYING ALL THE MEN ADORE ME AND TRYING TO
ENGAGE.
MY NAME IS CALLED OUT AS I TAKE ONE LAST LOOK,
THE MEN ARE CHANTING MY NAME AND THEY ARE
READY TO READ MY BODY LIKE A BOOK.
I SLOWLY MOVE THROUGH THE STREAMERS WITH THE
COLORFUL LIGHTS BOUNCING OFF OF ME,
THE MEN CANVASSING MY BODY WANTING MORE TO
SEE.
ROWDY MEN DANCE AND PRANCE TO THE STAGE,
TRYING THEIR BEST PICKUP LINES IN A DRUNKEN RAGE.
I GRAB THE POLE, CLIMB TO THE TOP AND SLOWLY
SLIDE ON DOWN,
MEN DROPPING THEIR DRINKS LIKE THEY ARE ABOUT
TO DROWN.

They chant my name Serene,
Watching all these men in their own vivid
Dreams.
It's funny to me how these men look,
All their eyes popped out from my visual book.
My tops flies off and I swirl it around the
room,
Sweeping my body all over the stage like a
broom.
My breasts are fully bare and all the men
stare,
Some come a little closer and some fall out of
their chair.
Tips are flying and a few stuffed in my garter,
But my dancing will be the only barter.
Men are yelling my name as I take another ride
on the poll,
I have all the eyes in the building under my
control.
I crawl away slowly to the edge showing off
my double d's,
Swinging them around crawling on my knees.
The guys are hooting with ecstasy filled heads,
A pleasant picture for them before they go to
their beds.
Money is piling up all over this platform,
My body is glistening, sticky and warm.
The music is thumping and pulsates my every
move,
A full night a head with much more to prove.

My breasts swing around as the pole dancing
delivers more eyes,
But I have one more thing for these men and
it's my show surprise.
I always pick out one man from the crowd,
Whoever can make the most noise and be real
loud.
I found a man and I grabbed my lip stick,
Bright red and reapplying it with a little flick.
I leaned over and planted a kiss on his cheek,
To get a little closer look at me and peek.
This man thanked me for the kiss and told me I
was the best,
I grabbed his face and let him motor boat my
chest!!!!

I See You Looking

I see you looking
Over there with your friends
Smiling right through me
Is it my ass?
Is it my tits?
That you want to rub tanning lotion all over
I bet you can't even walk over here
It looks like you have a chubby
I wish you did walk over here
I want to see your big dick looking at me
I'd invite you over for some play time
Come on cutie
Don't you see my provocative look?
You don't read well to woman's signs
Oh well looks like someone else might rub me
down
"Excuse me sir, can you rub this lotion all over
me?"
Your loss guy over there
Guess whose dick will be in my mouth later?

Hit The Switch

Go ahead and hit the switch
I'll pull the curtains too
The candles will be perfect
To see all the sexiness in you
Lock that door
Undress real slow
Come closer to me
I want to see you glow
Undo my belt
Get down on your knees
Pull my jeans down
You dirty tease
I know this isn't right
We are co-workers only
But it's a desired need
We are both real lonely
I've wanted to fuck your face for so long
I know we are both going to hell
Please don't say anything to anyone
Promise not to tell?
Grab my shaft
Lick it really slow
I want it glistening with your saliva
You know where I want it to go
Put it down your throat
Take it in real slow
Where do you want me to come?
When I have to go

I LOVE IT HOW YOUR MOUTH IS SO FULL
WATCHING YOUR MASCARA RUN
RAMMING YOUR FACE
UNTIL THE MORNING SUN
YOU HAVE NO IDEA
HOW LONG I WANTED TO DO THIS
PLEASE TAKE A BREAK AND GIVE ME A DEEP KISS
EVER SINCE DAY ONE IN THE OFFICE
WITH YOUR LITTLE MINI SKIRTS
THE WAY YOUR BREASTS WOULD ARRANGE
INSIDE OF YOUR SEXY SHIRTS
PLEASE TAKE ME IN AGAIN
ALL THE WAY IN YOUR MOUTH
I WILL TICKLE YOUR PUSSY DOWN SOUTH
I WANT YOU TO MOAN MY NAME
SINCE I AM YOUR BOSS
I WILL KEEP YOU WET
AND GIVE YOUR ASS A TOSS
I'M ABOUT TO CUM
I WANT TO SHOOT IT ON YOUR CHEST,
OH MY GOD!
THANK YOU HONEY, YOU ARE THE BEST.

SHE BIT HER LIP

WE LOCKED EYES
ACROSS THE BAR
TIME STOPPED
EARTH SHATTERING EMOTIONS ROLLED
HER EYES CONTINUED TO DANCE MY WAY
BITING AT HER BOTTOM LIP
AROUSAL STIRRED MY SKIN
I WINKED BACK
DRINKING MORE FROM MY CUP
SHE STARTED WALKING TO ME
SLIPPING OUT OF MY CHAIR TO GREET HER
GRABBING MY FACE IN HER HANDS SHE KISSED ME
DEEPLY
LIKE WARRIORS FIGHTING WITH TONGUES
INTRIGUING EMOTIONS POURED
PULLING AWAY WE LOCK EYES
GRABBING AT MY HANDS
STUFFING THEM IN HER PANTS
MY HANDS MEET HER MOIST LIPS
RUBBING HER LIPS BACK AND FORTH
SHE SIGHS WITH PLEASURE
TAKING MY HANDS OUT
SHE STUFFS MY FINGERS IN MY MOUTH
ENJOYING HER FLAVORS
NOT CARING WHO IS WATCHING
LIFTING HER TO MY CHAIR
UNBUTTONING AND LOWERING HER PANTS
SLOWLY KISSING AT HER INNER THIGHS

TASTING HER WETNESS
PEOPLE START TO CIRCLE AROUND US
WATCHING ME EAT HER DINNER
INTRIGUING TO MANY
TASTY FOR ME
SHE BECOMES WETTER AND WETTER
BEAUTIFUL MOISTURE IN MY MOUTH
LICKING MY LIPS
LOOKING AT HER FACE
HUNGRILY TASTING MORE OF HER FANCY FEAST
DELICIOUS TO MY TASTE BUDS
SHE CAME
SHE CAME HARD IN MY MOUTH
SHE CONVULSED ON THE BAR STOOL
EXHAUSTED
BARKEEPER, MAY I HAVE A NAPKIN?

UNDRESSED

SHE UNDRESSED BEFORE ME
EXPOSING HER DELICATE SKIN
MY MOUTH SALIVATED
MY MIND STARTED TURNING
MY TONGUE KISSED HER SKIN
AWAKENING HER AROUSAL
HER BREASTS GREETED MY LIPS
AS I GENTLY SUCKLED
OUR HANDS EXPLORED
GRABBING AT OUR FANTASIES
HER BED FILLED WITH ROSE PETALS
OUR EYES DANCED TO IT
WARMING UP THE BED WITH PASSION
DELIVERING AND IGNITING LOVE

So Deep

I want to
Be
Buried
So deep
Inside you
That
I can
Taste
Yesterdays
Dinner

NEIGHBOR

I SPIED ON MY NEIGHBOR
HER WINDOWS WERE ALWAYS OPEN
INVITING FOR MY EYES
SHE WOULD DANCE ALL NIGHT IN HER ROOM
RIPPING OFF HER CLOTHES
HER BREASTS WERE SO PRECIOUS
DELICATE LIKE SNOW
IT WAS JAW DROPPING
NATURE AND I WAS HER AUDIENCE
EVERY NIGHT WAS THE SAME ROUTINE
MY ERECTION ALWAYS GREW QUICKLY
MY HANDS WANDERED
WITHOUT REMORSE
I WANTED TO TASTE HER
SHE LOOKED SO BEAUTIFUL
PLAYING WITH HER BREASTS
LIKE SHE KNEW THERE WAS AN AUDIENCE
WISHING HER HANDS WERE MINE
A PERFECT MOVIE
I CONTINUED TO WATCH FOR MONTHS
IT WAS A FREE SHOW
I COULDN'T JUST WALK AWAY
IT WAS MY SECRET
SHE NEVER KNEW
BUT I LOST THAT BATTLE
GOING THROUGH TONS OF UNDERWEAR

LINGERING

LINGERING
WERE MY KISSES
LANDING ON YOUR SOFT SKIN
PERCOLATING DESIRES
YOUR TINY HAIRS DANCING ON YOUR NECK
POETRY WAS WRITTEN
ALL OVER YOU
BECAUSE
YOU ARE MY QUEEN
A BEAUTIFUL SPECIMEN
I'M DRIVEN TOWARDS YOU
BECAUSE
YOU ARE SIMPLY RAVISHING

To Do List

HONEY!!
CAN YOU
WRITE DOWN
THINGS ON TOMORROWS
TO DO LIST?
PLEASE?
I FILLED UP
THE ENTIRE PAGE
WITH
HER
HER
HER
HER
HER

Don't Move

You are my prisoner
I won't bite
Much!
Just watch me
Marinate your skin
With my tongue
Relax
Your body is about to glisten
With my moisture
Of love
Sinking into your pores
My love will seep
Into your veins
Surging your every movement
I control you now
Until you sweat out
My nectar!

EATING HER

I LOVE
EATING HER
WITH MY EYES
CONSUMED
IN MY MIND
DIGESTED
IN MY HEART
BREATHING IN
HER BEAUTIFUL
AURA

DETENTION

DETENTION NEVER FELT SO GOOD!
DON'T SAY A WORD
DON'T YOU DARE SPEAK
UNDO YOUR DRESS
EXPOSE YOUR ASS CHEEKS
LAY DOWN OVER THERE
TAKE OFF YOUR BRA
YOU ARE IN MY DETENTION
YOU DIS-OBEYED MY LAW
NOW IT'S TIME FOR YOU TO PAY
FOR YOUR DISRUPTIVE BEHAVIOR
MY TONGUE IS GLISTENING
LICKING EVERY INCH OF YOU I WILL SAVOR!
I WANT TO LOSE ALL MY SALIVA
I WANT IT TO PENETRATE INTO YOUR SKIN
I WANT TO BITE YOUR JOLLY RANCHER NIPPLES
WHEN DO YOU WANT ME TO BEGIN?
LET ME START RIGHT HERE
GO AHEAD AND WIGGLE THOSE TOES
THIS IS JUST THE BEGINNING
THIS WILL BE A LONG SHOW
I LOVE WATCHING YOU SQUIRM
WITH YOUR BEAUTIFUL MEAT THAT JIGGLES
YOU THINK YOU ARE BEING CUTE
MY TONGUE WILL PROVIDE MORE GIGGLES
I'M TIRED OF LOOKING AT YOU
IT'S TIME TO EAT
MY LIPS ARE HUNGRY FOR YOURS

They look like a fancy feast
Your lips look real swollen
Like a butterfly in flight
I'm ready to munch
I need your protein tonight
I start to lick and flick
Your moans engage
Slowly licking around your taco
Writing poetry on your skin page
Release your dripping honey
I demand you to do it now
Don't make me lick your butthole
I'll have you mooooing like a cow

SLOW HANDS

WORK THEM
ALL OVER ME
SLOWLY
INVESTIGATE MY CURVES
REBIRTH MY GOOSE BUMPS
LET MY TINY HAIRS DANCE
WORK YOUR WAY INTO MY SOUL
DELIVER ME WITH SHIVERS
DOWN MY SPINE
LET ME RECLINE
INTO A TRANCE
I WANT YOU TO IGNITE MY SKIN
MY DIRTY THOUGHTS
MY DEEP DESIRES
LET ME BE YOUR PLAYGROUND
CLIMB YOUR WAY ON ME
I WANT TO BE YOUR SCHOOL RECESS
TAKE ME WHEN YOU ARE READY
I WANT TO BE YOUR BUFFET!

NIBBLE

I WANT TO NIBBLE
ALL OVER YOU
LIKE A SUMMER TIME MOSQUITO
BITING AT YOUR FLESH
AT A MURKY SUNSET
SO EVERY TIME YOU ITCH
YOU THINK OF ME

I Kissed Her

I kissed her
Deep and passionately
My nerves gave in
It was perfect
It was delicious
The sounds were profound
Her tongue tasted my desire
I was complete
I was flushed
I was drunk
I kissed every inch of her lips
I left my mark within her skin
For her to remember
My heart raced
Her lips were so soft
A cushion to my soul
I slowly backed away
Our eyes opened
Smiles and dimples swarmed
Glistening lips
Deep sighs erupted
BEEP.....BEEP.....BEEP......BEEP......BEEP.
SHIT!!!!!
This was just a dream

Take Me

Take me
I'm yours
Disperse your love into me
I am your destiny
I am your now
Fulfill my needs
Time is of the essence
Just stain me with your love
I won't feel this forever
I need what you need
Let's make an intimate memory
May you shine on my skin
Let's embark on a flavorful journey
I seek you tonight
Tomorrow we will be gone
Vanished in the wind
Blown away in another direction
Just to be a memory
From our passionate one night stand

BORROWED LOVE

CAN I BORROW YOUR LOVE?
MY HEART IS BEATING SLOWLY
I HAVE NOBODY IN MY LIFE
WITH NO AFFECTION TO SHOW

I'VE WAITED FOR A LONG TIME
LONELINESS MAKES ME SHAKE
TEARS FILL MY FACE
MY FLOORS TURN INTO A LAKE

JUST TO HAVE YOU ONE NIGHT
TO FEEL A WOMAN'S TOUCH
TO FEEL SPECIAL INSIDE
SOMETHING MY ARMS CAN CLUTCH

WILL YOU MAKE LOVE TO ME?
SO MY LIFE CAN BE MORE DIVINE
I HATE BEING ALONE
I'M STEADILY ON A DECLINE

I NEED YOU
I KNOW YOU ARE MY BEST FRIEND
A NIGHT OF PASSION
MY HEART MAY BE ABLE TO MEND

IT WILL FEEL WONDERFUL
WHAT DO YOU SAY?
I CAN NEVER FIND LOVE
DEAD ENDS GET IN MY WAY

I HAVE THE CHARM
I HAVE THE DESIRE
SHOW ME A CONNECTION
I NEED SOMEONE LIKE YOU TO ADMIRE

SO YOU SAY YES?
I THANK YOU SO MUCH
I WILL BRING WINE AND CANDLES
I CAN'T WAIT TO FEEL YOUR SOFT TOUCH!

With Her Eyes

She kissed me with her eyes
My skin started to flush
I turned bright red
My heart fell to mush

Her eyes danced
Everywhere on my skin
She kept looking
She started to grin

I felt like desert
As she canvassed my being
Afraid to look
But my mind was agreeing

My blood was boiling
Sweat started to pour
Biting her finger
I think she wanted more

But we are strangers
Like random birds in the sky
Her appetite was huge
And I caught her eye

HER EYES DANCED TO THE EXIT
SHE GRABBED MY HAND
UNDER HER SPELL
WHAT DOES SHE HAVE PLANNED?

DEAR CLEAVAGE

EVERYDAY
YOU DESTROY ME
WALKING BY
MY EYES STRAIN
MY HEART PUMPS
GOOSE BUMPS FORM
I SALIVATE
IN MY MOUTH
DROOLING
LICKING MY LIPS
LIKE STEAK BEFORE ME
DELICIOUS
SOFT CLOUDS
BOUNCE INTO MY VISION
LUST FORMS IN MY EYES
CONCENTRATION DIMINISHES
FOCUSING
ON THOSE SOFT GLOBES
WALKING AWAY STUNNED
CONFUSED
IN A DAY DREAM OF PASSION
POWERFUL
EMOTIONAL
LUCID THOUGHTS
RUMMAGING IN
MY MIND

VIBRATOR

I'M ALONE TONIGHT
WITH MY NAKED SKIN
SLIPPING SLOWLY INTO THE HOT TUB
SOAKED WITH DIRTY THOUGHTS
WISHING YOU WERE HERE TO FILL ME
BUZZZZZZZ
OH THAT SOUND
THAT SOUND IS DELIGHT
AS THIS STEAM RISES
MY HANDS DROWN IN THE WATER
TENDRILS OF FINGERS WALK MY INNER THIGHS
VIBRATING MY SKIN
MY ACCESS POINT SLOWLY OPENS
WITH TWO FINGERS
A SIGH OF PLEASURE ERUPTS MY FACE
INSERTING THE BUZZ
DEEPER AND DEEPER
BUBBLES THRASH
MY LEGS SWIM WITH THE CURRENTS
IN AND OUT
MY BODY QUIVERS
JOLTS
TWITCHES
AS I INHIBIT SWEET CREAM
SLOWLY LEAVING MY BODY
REFRESHED
REVITALIZED
REPLENISHED

FIREPLACE FUCK

LET'S WATCH THE GLOW
ON YOUR SKIN
RIDING MY DICK
BUCKING AND SUCKING ON MY NECK
GLISTENING WITH FIRE EMBERS AROUND US
PASSION AND LUST
DELIVERING STEAM
PICTURES GLOWING ON THE WALLS
MOANS CRACK INTO THE FIREPLACE
SNAPPING
SLAPPING BODIES
HEARTS RACING
INTO
ECSTASY
AS WE SLOWLY RISE
SOAKED IN BLISS
RAW IN EMOTIONS
TONGUES DANCE
BREATHES DEEP
SWEET SWEAT
SHINING IN PLEASURE

I CAN'T WAIT

I CAN'T WAIT ANY LONGER
HIKE ME UP ON THE WASHER
NOBODY'S HERE
FUCK ME RAW
BITE MY TITTIES LIKE COTTON CANDY
PULL MY THONG TO THE SIDE
I WANT YOU IN ME
DEEP
VERY DEEP
FUCK ME NOW I SAID
I WANT THE CAMERAS TO BREAK
FROM OUR BODIES THRASHING

EAT MY PUSSY

MEOW
DO YOU HEAR ME PURRING?
I'M WET
SOAKED LIKE A POND
TASTE MY TACO
I WANT TO FEEL YOUR TONGUE
IN MY WALLS
RETRIEVE THE LUST INSIDE ME
DEVOUR MY LIPS
KISS THEM LIKE NEW YEARS
TASTE EVERYTHING YOU CAN REACH
MY LOVE IS YOURS
FLICK YOUR TONGUE
MAKE ME MOAN
FLUSH ME WITH YOUR LOVE
DEPLETE MY BURNING DESIRE

I SEE YOU

I SEE YOU
WATCHING ME
WHILE I FOLD LAUNDRY
IN THE NUDE
YOUR GRASS CUTTING
LOOKS UNEVEN
DO YOU LIKE WHAT YOU SEE?
WHAT ABOUT MY TITS?
I WISH YOU COULD SUCK ON THEM
I WONDER YOUR THOUGHTS
I WONDER IF THEY ARE DIRTY LIKE MINE
COME OVER ONE DAY
STOP LOOKING
START TAKING

MR. MAILMAN

YOU BRING ME MY MAIL
WHY DON'T YOU BRING ME YOUR DICK
YOU STUFF MAIL IN MY DOOR SLOT
TRY PUTTING YOUR DICK IN THERE
I'LL SUCK IT SO GOOD
I'VE ALWAYS FANTASIZED ABOUT YOU
MAYBE ONE DAY
I'LL TAKE THE MAIL
IN MY PUSSY

How Deep

How deep
Can you go?
I want you in me
All the way
I want to feel your balls
On my clit
Fill me with your pudding
After I sauce your shaft

DOGGY STYLE

BEND ME OVER
MAKE ME PURR
STUFF ME DEEP
MAKE MY SPEECH SLUR

RAM ME HARD
RAM ME FAST
BREAK MY BODY
PUT ME IN A CAST

MAKE ME SWEAT
MAKE ME CUM
OPEN MY MOUTH
STICK IN YOUR THUMB

DRAIN YOUR LOVE
STAIN MY SKIN
SLAP MY ASS
REPEAT AND BEGIN

FINGER ME

FINGER ME
USE YOUR BIGGEST ONE
WIGGLE IT AROUND
MY PLEASURE CANAL
HIT EVERY WALL
PUT ME OVER THE EDGE
GIVE ME THE COME HERE MOTION
SWIRL YOUR FINGERS IN ME
LET ME EXPLODE FROM YOUR TOUCH

DICK

I WANT IT IN MY MOUTH
LIKE A THERMOMETER FOR THE FLU
LET ME SWIRL YOUR TIP
THEN PUSH IT ON THROUGH

I WANT TO LICK IT GOOD
BACK AND FORTH LIKE A TYPE WRITER
MAKING YOU SQUIRM
MAKING YOUR BALLS A LITTLE LIGHTER

HOW DOES IT FEEL?
RAMMING THE BACK OF MY THROAT
WITH MY HEAD ROCKING?
FASTER THAN A SPEED BOAT

HOW DOES IT FEEL WHEN I SLURP?
OR WHEN MY MASCARA RUNS
I LOVE THE NOISES YOUR DICK MAKES
I'M NOT AN INNOCENT NUN

I LOVE WATCHING YOUR HEART RATE
AS IT POUNDS OUT YOUR CHEST
MY LIPS ARE WORKING OVERTIME
FOR THE SATISFACTION OF YOUR MESS

CUM BABY CUM
I KNOW YOU WANT TO EXPLODE
PUT IT ANYWHERE YOU WANT
I LOVE BIG LOADS

I KNOW YOU CAN'T HANDLE MUCH MORE
I SEE YOUR LEGS STARTING TO SHAKE
YOUR EYES ARE ROLLING
YOUR BALLS ARE ABOUT BAKED

SQUIRT SMACK SQUISH
I LOVE YOUR CREAM SAUCE
HOW DO I LOOK GLISTENING?
NOW GET BACK TO WORK BECAUSE I AM YOUR BOSS

I Want To Fuck Your Wife

I want to fuck your wife
I know you want to fuck mine
So Saturday night will work
Come over at nine

We can each have a room
I'll take the loft
Just so you can hear your wife moan
When I'm kissing her skin that's so soft

I love your wife's tits
You always talk about my wife's peach ass
This will be a great night
Once these fantasies pass

I can't wait to be smothered in your wife's tits
I guess you have wanted to lick my wife's ass
I'm ready for your wife's nipples
My wife has talked about you mowing her grass

My wife likes her ass licked
As you finger her with two
She likes tasting her own cum
She'll want that from you

You mentioned your wife likes to ride like a
Bronco
I don't have a problem with that

JUST TO FUCK HER ONE TIME
I'LL MAKE HER PURR LIKE A CAT

WE CAN MEET UP OUTSIDE IN THE HOT TUB LATER
SO WE CAN TALK ABOUT OUR NIGHT
WE CAN SHARE SOME WINE AND LAUGHS
AND THE POSSIBILITY OF MORE DELIGHT

DAMP

You make me
Damp
Every day I see you
Especially when you cut your grass
Shirtless
I sit in my window
Staring at you
My fingers crawl away
Inside my thongs
Wishing it was you
Thinking it was
Pushing deeper into pleasure
I wait for the day
You see me
So you can see how badly I want you

SIT ON MY FACE

SIT ON MY FACE
ROTATE LIKE A CLOCK
MOVE YOUR HIPS UP AND DOWN
LET YOUR CRADLE JUST ROCK

LET ME MOVE YOUR LIPS
WITH MY SPICY TONGUE
BATHE ME IN YOUR WETNESS
I WANT YOU TO HAVE SOME FUN

LET MY TONGUE PUSH DEEPER
INSIDE YOUR WET CANAL
WE ARE BEST FRIENDS ALREADY
WE ARE LIKELY TO BE PALS

I LOVE BEING SMOTHERED
BY YOUR MOUNDING JOY
SUFFOCATING IN YOUR SEXY SMELLS
I ALWAYS WANT TO BE YOUR TOY

COME HERE

COME HERE
COME CLOSER
WATCH ME DANCE ON THIS STAGE
DON'T BE AFRAID
LOOK AT ME
DON'T BE SHY
I'LL SHOW YOU A GREAT NIGHT
I WANT YOUR EYES ON ME
WATCH ME SLIDE AND CLIMB THIS POLE
WATCH MY TITS DANCE IN THE AIR
ENJOY MY BUTT CHEEKS JIGGLE IN YOUR FACE
WHAT'S YOUR FAVORITE SONG?
I'LL GRIND ALL OVER FOR YOU
I KNOW YOU HAVE DIRTY THOUGHTS ABOUT ME
DOES YOUR MOTHER KNOW YOU ARE HERE?

BABY SITTER

WHAT'S WRONG WITH ME?
MY BODY IS CHANGING
MY DICK IS GROWING
FOR MY BABY SITTER
SHE WATCHES MY YOUNGER BROTHER
WHILE I WATCH HER
SHE COMES OVER WITH LOW CUT SHORTS
TOPS WITH CLEAVAGE POPPING OUT
I DROOL
I STARE
AT HER GOLDEN SKIN
WHY AM I THINKING BAD THOUGHTS?
I CAN'T TAKE THIS ANYMORE
I LOST MY FOCUS
I'M NERVOUS
I'M SWEATING
MY HORMONES ARE BOILING
I HAVE TO GO
I HAVE TO RELIEVE MY STRESS
I HAVE TO DRAIN MY LUST
INTO THE TOILET

FOLLOW ME

FOLLOW ME
TO MY BEDROOM
WHERE YOUR FANTASIES WILL END
LET ME TIE YOUR WRISTS
LET ME DANCE AND TEASE YOU
WATCH ME UNDRESS BEFORE YOU
I WANT YOU TO WIGGLE IN ANTICIPATION
I WANT YOU TO DEMAND WHAT YOU WANT
WATCH EACH ARTICLE OF CLOTHING DROP OFF ME
I WANT TO SEE YOU SALIVATE
I'M YOUR BUFFET TONIGHT
YOU WON'T LEAVE HUNGRY
YOU WILL BE FULL OF LUST AND DESIRE FOR YOUR
FUTURE
YOU WILL LEAVE MY ROOM WITH DIGNITY
YOU WILL VENTURE OFF INTO MAN HOOD
I KNOW YOU ARE A VIRGIN
I KNOW YOU ARE SHY
I KNOW YOU HAVE DARK FANTASIES
DRAIN ALL YOUR THINKABLE DESIRES ON ME
ARE YOU READY FOR ME TO FUCK YOUR BRAINS OUT?

BUFFET

TREAT
ME LIKE
A BUFFET
NIBBLE ON EVERY CURVE
TASTE THE EDGES OF MY SKIN
SAVOR MY MEATY LOINS
WASH ME DOWN
WITH MY MOISTURE
SECRETING
DRIPPING
LEAKING INTO YOUR PALATE
AS MY DESIRE
SEEPS SLOWLY DOWN YOUR
THROAT

"CONQUER YOUR DESIRES, ONE DIRTY THOUGHT AT A TIME"

K.J.A

81848713R00097

Made in the USA
Lexington, KY
22 February 2018